STUDENT MOTIVATION

Cultivating a Love of Learning

Linda Lumsden

Foreword by Catherine Lewis

ERIC Clearinghouse on
Educational Management

University of Oregon
1999

Library of Congress Cataloging-in-Publication Data
Lumsden, Linda S..

    Student motivation : cultivating a love of learning / Linda Lumsden
       p. cm.

    Includes bibliographical references (p.).

    ISBN 0-86552-141-7

    1. Motivation in education—United States. 2. Classroom environment—United States. 3. School environment—United States.

    I. Title.
    LB1065.L86 1999
    370.15'4—dc21   99-20577

                                                                                                         CIP

Design: LeeAnn August
Type: 10.5/12 Palatino
Printer: Publishers Press, Salt Lake City, Utah
E1970

Printed in the United States of America, 1999

ERIC Clearinghouse on Educational Management
    5207 University of Oregon
    Eugene, OR 97403-5207
    Telephone: (541) 346-5044 Fax: (541) 346-2334
    World Wide Web: http://eric.uoregon.edu
ERIC/CEM Accession Number: EA 029 566

This publication was prepared in part with funding from the Office of Educational Research and Improvement, U.S. Department of Education, under contract no. OERI-RR 93002006. The opinions expressed in this report do not necessarily reflect the positions or policies of the Department of Education. No federal funds were used in the printing of this publication.

The University of Oregon is an equal opportunity, affirmative action institution committed to cultural diversity.

MISSION OF ERIC AND THE CLEARINGHOUSE

The Educational Resources Information Center (ERIC) is a national information system operated by the U.S. Department of Education. ERIC serves the educational community by disseminating research results and other resource information that can be used in developing more effective educational programs.

The ERIC Clearinghouse on Educational Management, one of several such units in the system, was established at the University of Oregon in 1966. The Clearinghouse and its companion units process research reports and journal articles for announcement in ERIC's index and abstract bulletins.

Research reports are announced in *Resources in Education* (*RIE*), available in many libraries and by subscription from the United States Government Printing Office, Washington, D.C. 20402-9371.

Most of the documents listed in *RIE* can be purchased through the ERIC Document Reproduction Service, operated by Cincinnati Bell Information Systems.

Journal articles are announced in *Current Index to Journals in Education*. *CIJE* is also available in many libraries and can be ordered from Oryx Press, 4041 North Central Avenue at Indian School, Suite 700, Phoenix, Arizona 85012. Semiannual cumulations can be ordered separately.

Besides processing documents and journal articles, the Clearinghouse prepares bibliographies, literature reviews, monographs, and other interpretive research studies on topics in its educational area.

CLEARINGHOUSE NATIONAL ADVISORY BOARD

Terry A. Astuto, Vice-President, Division A, American Educational Research Association

George Babigian, Executive Director, American Education Finance Association

Anne L. Bryant, Executive Director, National School Boards Association

Patrick Forsyth, Executive Director, University Council for Educational Administration

Paul Houston, Executive Director, American Association of School Administrators

John T. MacDonald, Director, State Leadership Center, Council of Chief State School Officers

Philip K. Piele, (Chair), Professor and Director, ERIC Clearinghouse on Educational Management, University of Oregon

Samuel G. Sava, Executive Director, National Association of Elementary School Principals

Gerald Tirozzi, Executive Director, National Association of Secondary School Principals

ADMINISTRATIVE STAFF

Philip K. Piele, Professor and Director
Stuart C. Smith, Associate Director

CONTENTS

Acknowledgments vii

Foreword ix

Introduction 1

Chapter 1: What Is Student Motivation? 7
    Ways of Conceptualizing Student Motivation 9
    Some Factors That Affect Student Motivation To Learn 15
    Conclusion 26

Chapter 2: Caring and High Expectations: Cornerstones of Motivation 29
    A Sense of Caring and Connection 30
    How Caring Can Be Conveyed in the School Setting 33
    Maintaining High Expectations 43
    Conclusion 47

Chapter 3: Perspectives of Practitioners 49
    Ted Nussbaum, Eugene, Oregon 50
    Cindy Boyd, Abilene, Texas 53
    Howard Pitler, Wichita, Kansas 59
    Conclusion 64

Chapter 4: Classroom Considerations 65
    A Supportive, Respectful Climate 66
    Deemphasizing Competition 69
    Responsibility and Choice 71
    Meaning, Relevance, and Teaching Methods 72
    Task Difficulty 77
    Variety 78
    Instructive Feedback 80
    Student Self-Evaluation 80

    Attention to Both Mind and Character 82
    Positive Peer Relations 83
    Look to Students for Input 86
    Conclusion 87

Chapter 5: Schoolwide Strategies 89
    Schoolwide Learning Goals 90
    Organization of Curriculum 100
    Conclusion 103

Conclusion 107

Bibliography 109

ACKNOWLEDGMENTS

Without the assistance, involvement, and influence of several people, I am certain this endeavor would never have come to fruition. The following individuals, each in his or her own way, helped to coach me through the many labor pains I experienced during the birthing of this book. To all of you I offer my gratitude and heartfelt thanks:

> Stuart Smith for his adept oversight of the project, excellent editorial input, confidence in my capacity to see the project through, and discipline to wait patiently
>
> JoAnn Mazzarella for offering organizational guidance, graciously agreeing to read the manuscript, and providing astute feedback
>
> LeeAnn Agost for gracing the book with her graphic design skills, giving me a sense of camaraderie, keeping me laughing, and accompanying me on my all too frequent trips to the bakery
>
> Dr. Susan Moseley for listening with the heart as well as the head, offering steadfast support, and practicing therapeutic artistry
>
> Dr. Vicki Collins for her words of encouragement, prayers, and appreciation of the complexity of the subject
>
> Sheryl Fortin for her faithful friendship and consistent willingness to lend an ear
>
> Kathryn Nelson Albere for sensing and giving what is needed and for always touching base at just the right time
>
> George, Joyce, Barb, and Lee Lumsden for their love and for setting a standard of excellence through their facility with the written word

Bill and Barb Winter and their daughters Maryann, Katherine, and Jane for being there when I needed them, believing in me, and extending both their heart and home

Jason Moran for teaching me much about myself and about motivation to learn

To others whom I may have inadvertently neglected to mention, my apologies. Abundant appreciation is extended to you as well.

FOREWORD

Motivation: Perhaps no other quality is so important to success in school, nor so misunderstood. In casual conversation, we often talk about motivation as if it is something that can be pushed and pulled from the outside, as in "How can we motivate him?" or "These prizes are good motivators." In this volume, Linda Lumsden goes beyond such "quick fix" notions to explain how motivation is the ultimate product of many aspects of the school experience: significant relationships between teachers and students and among students; a meaningful, well-taught curriculum; teachers who maintain high expectations and look for ways to help each student connect to the curriculum; opportunities for choice and self-evaluation that foster students' ownership of learning.

This book makes the case that young children's natural motivation to learn will survive only in schools where the curriculum is worth learning and teachers help students see why it is worth learning; where students focus on *learning* (not on competition or grades); and where students feel valued, and therefore are disposed to care about the school's values, including learning. In other words, the job of schools is to help students develop a commitment to learning that sustains them even when a particular task seems too difficult or unappealing. They are most likely to develop this commitment in a school that meets their needs for belonging, contribution, and meaningful work.

When I think back on my own elementary education in the late 1950s, I cannot think of an aspect of educational practice (except use of computers) that has changed more than techniques of "motivation." As a child, I had never heard of prizes for good behavior, table points, pizza for reading books, or time out. These practices are widespread now, despite evidence that, in the long run, they are likely to *undermine* students' commitment to learning and to responsible behavior. Recent research suggests that practitioners who shift away from systems of rewards and punishment and, instead, actively involve students in shaping classroom climate and learning (through methods such as class meetings) promote both students' motivation to learn and their commitment to democratic values (D. Solomon and others forthcoming; Catherine Lewis forthcoming).

Is it our increasingly impersonal, mobile society that has pushed us to emphasize carrots and sticks, rather than rely on the motivation that naturally arises in significant, valued relationships with teachers and fellow students? Are current students less easily brought into such significant relationships? Or do we fail to invest adequate time in nurturing such relationships within our schools? Given the pressure on both educators and students to attend to test scores, supportive human relationships may seem like an amenity we cannot afford. Research reviewed in this volume suggests, however, that carrots and sticks, while they may produce short-term results, simply won't produce the self-motivated learners our society needs.

My ideas about motivation were shaken up about twenty years ago, when I first began to study Japanese elementary schools. (I both read and speak Japanese.) Missing, from both Japanese childrearing at home and preschool and elementary education, are the rewards and consequences that are now commonplace in U.S. schools — stickers, points, names on board, time-outs, emphasis on grades. Instead, Japanese elementary teachers focus their attention on building close, supportive relationships and involving children in classroom management (Catherine Lewis 1995).

Even at first grade, Japanese students run class meetings, set personal goals, self-evaluate their behavior, and discuss "the kind of class we want to be." They form class "promises" and goals based on their class discussion. During twice-daily class meetings, Japanese students regularly assess their progress toward becoming, for example, "a friendly class that works hard at learning." Students, not teachers, call the class together for each lesson and after recess and lunch, and this responsibility (which rotates through all class members in order, without regard to their ability or behavior) regularly places even the most obstreperous children in a position of authority. When problems arise, they are discussed and solved by students, with teachers helping students to remember the virtues of kindness, responsibility, and helpfulness they hope will guide school life (Lewis 1995).

Equally striking is the emphasis, in Japanese elementary schools, on forging close, supportive relationships among students and between students and teachers. Teachers typically spend two years with the same class, and about thirty days of the famed longer Japanese school year are spent in whole-school activities (for example, school trips, hiking, arts festival, sports festival) designed to build a feeling of community within the school (Lewis 1995). Educators do not just "happen" to emphasize human relationships: One goal of Japan's national *Course of Study* is for students to develop "intimacy with classmates and an enjoyment of classroom life."

Rewards and punishments are conspicuously absent from Japanese elementary classrooms, and teachers rely on students' interest in well-taught, important subject matter, *self*-evaluation, and enjoyment of group life to gradually build discipline and support motivation to learn. As one Japanese teacher said when asked why she didn't use rewards, "Even for a dog, it is humiliating to do tricks in the hope of getting something for it." Other teachers explained that rewards were used only as a last resort, when there was no relationship between student and teacher to build from. The assumption by Japanese educators that motivation grows from strong, valued human relationships and opportunities to shape the classroom environment shook up my thinking.

Similarly, this book has the potential to shake up our thinking and help us take a fresh look at the diverse aspects of school life that shape motivation. After reading this volume, it will be hard to think about "motivation" without seeing it as the very heart of education, and without thinking about the important, well-taught curriculum, close, supportive relationships, and high expectations that are its foundation. If your thinking is shaken up and you want to bring to life in the classroom and school the much more ambitious, long-term view of motivation this volume describes, additional resources can be found at the end of the volume.

Catherine Lewis
Developmental Studies Center
Oakland, California

INTRODUCTION

Human beings are born with a hunger to learn, a seemingly insatiable appetite for knowledge. Infants and young children appear to be propelled by curiosity, driven by an innate need to explore, interact with, and make sense of their environment. As one author notes, "Rarely does one hear parents complain that their preschooler is 'unmotivated' " (James Raffini 1993).

It is unfortunate that as children progress through our educational system, learning—at least learning that occurs in school settings—often becomes associated with drudgery rather than delight. Many toddlers who immerse themselves in exploring almost anything and everything around them later become "turned off" by the educational system. Somewhere along the line they seem to lose their love of learning.

Figures on dropout rates are one window into the problem of student disaffection with school. Tragically, each year 500,000 students in the U.S. leave school "without diplomas or life skills" (Hillery Motsinger 1993). But the apparent absence of motivation to learn is not confined to students who leave school prematurely.

Many who remain in school also exude apathy. These students seem content with "sliding by," doing the minimum possible to get advanced to the next grade level. They show little interest in, and devote little time or energy to, school-related tasks. As a result, their achievement falls well below their ability. As Raffini notes, "More than one in four students who enter first grade leave before graduating, and many of those who do continue avoid making a personal commitment to the learning process."

Therefore, in addition to being concerned with how motivational problems contribute to student dropout rates, we must also address the issue of why a large portion of those students who stay in school fail to invest themselves fully in the experience of learning. Apathetic students will be less likely to achieve their full potential than those who manage to retain a sense of excitement and satisfaction about learning for its own sake.

Raymond Wlodkowski and Judith Jaynes (1990) are among those who note the correlation between motivation and underachievement. They state that

> since 1980 more than a dozen reports from national panels and commissions that have studied public education in this country agree that the school achievement of our children is below their abilities. In all of these instances, one of the main reasons cited is that many of our children lack motivation to learn in school.

But has the problem of student disengagement really been growing or is awareness of it merely increasing? Apparently disengagement and lack of motivation are more widespread than in the past. Laurence Steinberg (1996) asserts that there has been an upward shift in the proportions of disengaged students over the past twenty-five years.

> Teachers have always encountered students who were difficult to interest and hard to motivate, but the number of these students was considerably smaller in the past than it is today. Two decades ago, a teacher in an average high school in this country could expect to have three or four "difficult" students in a class of thirty. Today, teachers in these same schools are expected to teach to classrooms in which nearly half of the students have "checked out." (Steinberg)

The widespread disengagement of America's students is a problem with enormous implications and profound potential consequences. Although it is less visible, less dramatic, and less commented upon than other social problems involving youth—such as drug and alcohol use, pregnancy, and violence—student disengagement is more pervasive and in some ways potentially more harmful to the future well-being of American society.

As Steinberg emphasizes, the fallout from student disenchantment with school is far-reaching. While a multitude of factors contribute to students' mental and physical exodus from our nation's school system, most educators and researchers agree that when students become disconnected from a desire to learn, they are at much greater risk of either severing their relationship with the formal educational system or remaining in school but failing to achieve their full potential. There are also long-term personal and professional repercussions for individuals who do not successfully negotiate their way through our educational system. Our country as a whole also pays an economic and social price for students' languishing motivation to learn.

Student engagement not only has implications for educational achievement and future occupational attainment but may also reflect students' general psychological and social health. Since attending school is one of the few responsibilities all children are expected to fulfill, and success in school is one of the few values nearly all parents attempt to impart to their children, students' level of engagement in school can be viewed as a broad barometer of their willingness to adopt or internalize not only values related to education but a range of other values widely held by adult society (Steinberg). That is, students who reject education as a relevant value may be more likely to reject other values and precepts embraced by a majority of citizens.

Interest in school tends to serve as a "buffer" against psychological problems (Steinberg). Students with high interest and involvement in school "score higher on measures of psychological adjustment, such as assessments of self-esteem, responsibility, and competence in social relationships" (Steinberg).

On the other hand, disengagement from school is associated with a host of psychological and behavioral problems. According to Steinberg,

> Youngsters who are disengaged from school are far more likely than their peers to use and abuse drugs and alcohol, fall prey to depression, experiment with early sex, and commit acts of crime and delinquency. For these reasons, understanding the causes and correlates

of children's engagement in school helps us better understand the forces in their lives that affect all aspects of their behavior and well-being, not just their performance on tests of school achievement.

Teachers consistently identify the issue of student motivation as one of their chief concerns (Carole Ames 1990). They want to know more about such things as how to motivate students who appear disengaged from and disinterested in learning, how to help students value learning for its own sake, and how to develop a motivating classroom "personality" or climate.

Unfortunately, the subject of motivation receives scant attention at most teacher training institutions. Teachers usually enter the classroom with an inadequate foundation in both motivational theory and classroom application of motivational principles. They are often left to rely on their intuition to guide them in motivational matters. However, many motivational principles are actually "counterintuitive," which means that the compass of "conventional wisdom" cannot be counted upon to reliably guide teachers through challenging motivational terrain (Ames 1990).

While classroom teachers are instrumental in shaping students' motivational patterns, written and unwritten goals and values that permeate the "culture" of the school are also influential. Although teachers can do much at the classroom level to stimulate students' involvement in and enjoyment of learning, their efforts will be diminished if school-level policies, procedures, and values run counter to those at the classroom level. For example, if the relative standing of students is emphasized at the school level, this schoolwide value will subvert teachers' attempts to focus on individual effort and progress and downplay competition and comparisons across students.

Although teachers and school leaders influence the course of student motivation, parents also play a pivotal, enduring role in shaping their children's attitudes toward learning. After children enter school, the level of parent involvement in their children's education becomes very important. However, attitudes toward learning begin to take root in children long before they ever set foot in a school building. When they are still toddlers, children begin to pick up powerful messages about learning based on the way their parents respond to their innate curiosity about the world.

Whether children are raised by parents who provide them with a basic sense of self-worth and self-efficacy also influences students' attitudes toward learning. Children who have low self-esteem are generally more psychologically vulnerable in the face of failure than are children who possess a solid sense of self-esteem. Whenever possible, children with low self-esteem are inclined to avoid academic challenges and the risks inherent in learning because the prospect of failure is so threatening to their fragile sense of self-worth.

Another way parents influence their children is through the transmission of values. If parents value learning for its own sake and this value is evident in their everyday lives, perhaps through activities such as pleasure reading or the pursuit of various hobbies, their children are more likely to cherish learning.

Finally, as we attempt to unravel, at least partially, the enigma of motivation to learn, the perceptions of students themselves must not be left out of the equation. When consulted and given a voice, students have much to say about what they need to support their quest to learn and grow.

This book examines student motivation from a practical as well as a theoretical perspective. Why children's passion for learning frequently seems to shrink as they grow—and what to do to prevent or reverse this trend—is one of its central themes. It examines approaches to nurturing and reviving student motivation at the classroom level and the school level, and considers students' perspectives on learning and motivation.

Chapter 1 provides a glimpse at some of the theoretical underpinnings of student motivation through the examination of several motivation-related terms and concepts. Caring and high expectations, two cornerstones of motivation, are examined in chapter 2. Chapter 3 presents a sampling of practitioners' perspectives about student motivation gleaned from interviews. Chapter 4 discusses elements at a classroom level that may affect student motivation. Finally, chapter 5 focuses on aspects of school-level structure, policy, and practice that may impede or promote motivation and engagement of students.

1

WHAT IS STUDENT MOTIVATION?

There are three things to remember about education. The first one is motivation. The second one is motivation. The third one is motivation.
—former U.S. Secretary of Education
Terrell H. Bell (in Raffini)

Nearly all decisions about schooling, whether made in the school board chamber, the central office, the principal's office, or the classroom—even decisions about policies and procedures that seem remotely related to instruction and learning—have an effect, intended or not, on students' motivation to learn. Without some grounding in motivational concepts and how they apply to the classroom, however, administrators, educators, and policymakers may remain unaware of the motivational implications of many of their decisions.

Teachers' daily interactions with students enable them to most directly shape students' attitudes. But if teachers have not been schooled in motivational principles, they will lack a framework to guide them in selecting activities that will foster "long-term and high-quality involvement in learning" (Carole Ames 1992). Teachers may also fail to recognize or attend to other aspects of classroom environment that affect the way in which students approach and engage in academic activities.

True, students bring their preexisting motivational patterns to the classroom, but they are not beyond change. Teachers who possess an understanding of some of the dynamics that affect students' motivation to learn are able to act as *"active socialization agents* capable of stimulating the general development of student motivation to learn and its activation in particular situations" (Jere Brophy 1987) [Emphasis in original].

Beyond the classroom, school-level policies and practices also affect student motivation to learn. If administrators do not understand motivational principles, they may initiate, with good intentions, learning goals at the school level that actually undermine teachers' more constructive efforts in the classroom. What message will students act on, for example, if teachers try to impress on them the value of effort, improvement, and active engagement in learning while the principal promotes a program to reward a few students for their outstanding performance relative to other students?

Of course, the same problem holds if the roles are reversed. Teachers who overtly or covertly reinforce norms of competition can subvert principals' schoolwide focus on the inherent value of learning. To instill in students an appreciation for learning, teachers and administrators must act in concert, their efforts complementing each other.

Of even greater importance for students' motivation to learn is teamwork between school personnel and parents. When children are affirmed and encouraged both at home and at school to take an interest in learning, the more likely they will be to value learning for its own sake rather than for any external rewards they may reap. If, however, the messages students receive at home and at school differ, students are likely to be confused about which set of learning-related values and beliefs to adopt. Clear communication between home and school, and partnerships between parents and teachers, can go a long way toward keeping students motivated to learn.

Granted, there is "no magic solution to the problem of student motivation" (Donald Grossnickle and William Thiel 1988). Much has been learned in recent years, however, about the nature of student motivation and about how to adapt students' motivational patterns. This chapter discusses some motivation-related terms prevalent in the literature and then discusses some factors that affect students' basic beliefs about and attitudes toward learning.

Ways of Conceptualizing Student Motivation

Student motivation is a complex, multidimensional concept. Lyn Corno (1992) mentions some elements associated with student motivation:

> Motivation to accomplish goals, expressed interest in and effort toward schoolwork, self-confidence in one's own ability, and persistence in the face of difficulty—these are aspects of motivation most of us call to mind in the academic arena, and all are theoretically important.

Basically, student motivation has to do with the reasons students engage—or in some cases choose not to engage—in school-related academic endeavors. It is related to what provides the impetus for students' participation in the learning process. When attempting to unravel the mystery of student motivation, it is essential to try to tease out *why* students undertake learning. Two students may each elect to pursue the same task, but their reasons for doing so may be as different as night and day.

It is helpful for teachers to have a sense of the primary reasons that prompt individual students to pursue academic activities, because these underlying reasons "have important consequences for how [students] approach and engage in learning" (Ames 1990). Students whose paramount goal is a good grade will engage in thought processes and behaviors that are likely to differ from those of students who are interested in learning something new about a subject (Ames 1990). As Corno notes, "Students who are generally inclined to approach schoolwork from the point of learning and mastering the material (so-called learning/mastery orientations) tend to differ in work styles from students whose goals or intentions generally lead from the other point, that is, to obtain grades or display competence."

Extrinsic Versus Intrinsic Orientation

Much of the literature on student motivation refers to two basic learning orientations. Depending on why they pursue learning tasks, students are said to be primarily *intrinsically oriented* or *extrinsically oriented*. Mark Lepper

(1988) states that intrinsically motivated behavior is "undertaken for its own sake, for the enjoyment it provides, the learning it permits, or the feelings of accomplishment it evokes." In contrast, extrinsically motivated behavior consists of "actions undertaken *in order to* obtain some reward or avoid some punishment external to the activity itself" [Emphasis in original].

Those with an extrinsic orientation toward learning perform school-related tasks primarily because they view them as a means of obtaining some form of reward not integral to the tasks themselves (that is, they may be striving for good grades or stickers or a place on the school honor roll). Those who have an intrinsic motivational orientation perceive learning as a process that has inherent value and meaning.

Mastery Goals Versus Performance Goals

Mastery goals and *performance goals* are two other terms frequently used to characterize students' motivational orientations (Ames 1992). The two categories represent "different conceptions of success and different reasons for approaching and engaging in achievement activity" (Ames 1992). A student who is motivated by mastery goals focuses on "developing new skills, trying to understand their work, improving their level of competence, or achieving a sense of mastery based on self-referenced standards" (Ames 1992).

Students who possess mastery goals believe that effort leads to success or mastery; they also spend more time on learning tasks and display higher levels of persistence in the face of failure. In addition, students motivated by mastery goals tend to prefer challenging work and willingly engage in academic risk-taking (Carole Ames and Jennifer Archer 1988).

In contrast, when performance goals take precedence, students do not focus on the learning activity itself; instead, they concentrate primarily on how their performance on a task will reflect on their perceived ability and sense of self-worth. They view ability, rather than effort, as the strongest determinant of outcome. These students have an especially strong need to be perceived as able, and they think of ability in terms of doing better than others, exceeding normative standards, and experiencing success with minimal effort (Ames 1992).

Students who are performance-oriented seek public acknowledgment that they have performed at a higher level than others, that they have displayed superior ability. Those with this orientation view learning as a means to an end, not an end in itself. Their self-concept of ability, so intimately entwined with and potentially threatened by their performance, has an impact on how they cope with academic tasks. If they see failure as probable, they often prefer to withhold effort than to try hard and risk failure, because if they don't put forth effort their failure cannot be attributed to lack of ability.

Although theoretically students are classified in an "either/or" fashion (as being intrinsically or extrinsically oriented or having mastery or performance goals), in reality the division cannot be so easily drawn. That is, students are not generally purely intrinsically or extrinsically oriented. Rather, to varying degrees, intrinsic and extrinsic factors motivate most students just as they motivate most individuals in the workplace (that is, a person may find his job personally satisfying but would not necessarily continue to come to work if a paycheck were not forthcoming at the end of every month).

In addition, what motivates students is not likely to be static across all types of tasks. Depending on the nature of the task they are asked to perform, students may be relatively more or less motivated by intrinsic or extrinsic factors. In one situation intrinsic factors may be the primary motivators, while in another situation extrinsic elements could be preeminent. Although for the sake of clearly distinguishing terms associated with motivation to learn it may make sense to refer to students as having one motivational orientation or the other, real students are multidimensional, complex human beings motivated by a multitude of factors.

Benefits of an Intrinsic Motivational Orientation

One might ask, Why does it matter whether a student leans toward one motivational orientation or the other? If students complete the tasks that educators set before them, isn't that the bottom line? Shouldn't we concentrate on students who seem to have completely lost their appetite for formal learning activities—those who can't seem to find any reason to invest themselves in school-related tasks?

Without question it is crucial for educators to understand why some students become severely disengaged from and apathetic toward school, to decipher why, as Raffini puts it, many students "reject school as a valued activity." However, it is equally important for teachers to nurture intrinsic motivation to learn in all students. This is essential because a growing body of evidence suggests that the way students approach tasks, the cognitive and affective processes they employ, and the level of learning that they ultimately derive from undertaking tasks depend to a great extent on whether students are operating from an extrinsic or an intrinsic motivational orientation.

Behaviors and Effects Associated with Motivational Orientation

One's motivational orientation can affect both the time spent on a task and the quality of involvement in the task (Lepper). Of these two variables, Ames (1990) would argue that the quality of involvement is the more important one. As she notes, information that can be derived from students' time on task is limited. We cannot, by looking at time-on-task in isolation, be certain about what students are attending to, how they are processing information, how they are reacting to their performance, and how they are interpreting feedback. What is critical, Ames says, "is the quality of engaged time, not the duration of engaged time."

Motivational orientation can also have a bearing on the level of task difficulty students select (Lepper). Students with an intrinsic orientation tend to prefer tasks that are moderately challenging, whereas extrinsically oriented students gravitate toward tasks that are low in degree of difficulty. The latter will be most concerned with doing only what is necessary to obtain some form of reward that is external to the task itself. Extrinsically oriented students are also less likely than internally oriented students to take academic risks as they respond to a given task (Lepper).

Generally, individuals with an extrinsic orientation toward learning tend to expend less mental effort and employ less deliberate and less effective strategies when undertaking an activity than do intrinsically oriented individuals. Susan Bobbitt Nolen (1988), for example, found that students' motivational orientation influenced the types of strategies they valued and employed when studying or performing an activity. Students who engaged in expository reading with the primary goal of learning for its own sake (intrinsic motivation) tended to value and use study strategies that demanded more effort and that enabled them to process information more deeply. In contrast, students who were primarily driven by the desire to demonstrate that they had superior ability at the task relative to other students (a form of extrinsic motivation) put forth less mental effort.

Similarly, J. Condry and J. Chambers (1978) found that when students were confronted with complex intellectual tasks, those with an intrinsic motivational orientation used more logical information-gathering and decision-making strategies than did students who were extrinsically oriented.

Student Motivation To Learn

The concepts of *student motivation to learn* and *intrinsic motivational orientation* are closely related. Although some authors seem to view them as essentially synonymous, others do not. The idea of involvement in academic tasks for internal reasons, such as personal benefits the learner derives from the learning experience, is integral to both terms. Both terms also can be used when describing learning that is undertaken primarily for the personal benefits it brings to the learner rather than for the purpose of meeting various forms of external demands or expectations.

Jere Brophy (1986) is among those who define the terms differently. If a student tends to find meaning and value in school-related activities, and tries to get "the intended academic benefits" from those activities, Brophy would say the student possesses *motivation to learn*. Intrinsic motivation, on the other hand, "usually refers to the affective aspects of motivation—liking for or enjoyment of an activity," states Brophy. When this distinction is made, it is possible for motivation to learn to be present even when enjoyment is absent. Although students may not find an activity particularly pleasurable, they can still strive to get the intended benefits or meaning from them.

Educators interested in promoting motivation to learn should focus on helping students to "develop goals, beliefs, and attitudes... [that] will contribute to quality involvement in learning" (Ames 1990). To get a sense of the status of motivation in their classrooms, teachers should evaluate "whether students initiate learning activities and maintain an involvement in learning as well as a commitment to the process of learning" (Ames 1990).

Achievement and Performance

Although motivation is related to achievement, valid inferences about motivation cannot be made by examining achievement data (Ames 1990). Motivation to learn must be seen as a worthy outcome apart from its potential to enhance achievement (Ames 1990). If teachers and school leaders promote motivation to learn only as a means to the ultimate goal of increased achievement, they may not notice or even be particularly concerned that some practices that produce short-term gains in achievement also erode motivation. If achievement is stressed at all costs, teachers may fail to nurture in students the types of goals, beliefs, and attitudes that will enable them to engage fully in, and derive enjoyment and satisfaction from, learning (Ames 1990).

Similarly, Brophy points out the necessity of distinguishing *learning* from *performance*. While performance is overt in that it refers to the demonstration of skills or knowledge, the learning process is primarily covert; it consists of activities such as "information-processing, sense-making, and comprehension." When seeking to support or enhance motivation to learn, then, we should be concerned not only with strategies that have the capacity to enhance students' abilities to take tests and complete assignments, but with strategies that support and strengthen students' information-processing activities, such as paying attention, reading for understanding, paraphrasing, and so forth.

Some Factors That Affect Student Motivation To Learn

Motivation to learn does not exist in a vacuum; many factors influence the initial constellation of attitudes children develop toward learning. Subsequent experiences that students have as they pass through the educational system either affirm or alter their evolving motivational patterns and associations with learning.

The Role of Parents

As Wlodkowski and Jaynes note, parents model and interpret the world to their children; they are "the first and most important teachers in a child's life." At least when they are young, most children tend to view the world in much the same way that their parents do.

Children's initial associations with learning are primarily an outgrowth of what they experience and observe in their home environment. With learning as with other areas, children pick up on the subtle and not-so-subtle attitudes and values that are held by their parents.

When parents nurture their children's natural curiosity about the world by welcoming their questions, encouraging exploration, and familiarizing them with resources that can enlarge their world (such as the library), they are giving their children the message that learning is a worthwhile endeavor, and that it is also frequently fun and satisfying. If, on the other hand, parents are consistently unresponsive or react with irritation or impatience when their children inquire about things that intrigue them, over time their children will probably curb their attempts to learn more about the world. Their natural interest in learning will probably begin to wane, at least until someone crosses their path who skillfully "primes the pump" by creating a climate in which the child's dormant desire to learn once again bubbles to the surface.

In addition to whether parents are responsive to their children's cognitive needs and supply them with developmentally appropriate forms of cognitive stimulation, the degree to which parents provide their children with a basic sense of emotional security also influences their children's confidence in learning and motivation to learn. If children lack a solid sense of their own worth, competence, and self-efficacy—in short, if children do not learn to believe in themselves—their freedom to engage in academically challenging pursuits and capacity to tolerate and cope with failure will be greatly diminished. The attitudes and beliefs students have about themselves play a significant role in determining whether they develop constructive or ultimately self-defeating motivation patterns.

Parents' own attitudes toward school and education also come into play. If parents' school-related experience was predominantly negative, they may find it hard to view their children's teachers as potential allies. It is regrettable but understandable that parents whose own school experience left a bad taste in their mouths are probably not going to perceive their children's teachers as partners. The pain some parents carry from their own negative school experiences as children may cloud their vision and make it difficult for them to see their own children's educational experience objectively, particularly if it does not confirm their deep-seated preexisting beliefs. They are likely to distrust or be intimidated by school personnel and shy away from direct involvement in their children's formal education.

Conversely, parents who had a positive educational experience during their childhood and place a premium on formal education are more likely to think of school and teachers in a positive light. They are apt to initiate a relationship with school personnel and assume, even demand, a high level of participation and involvement in their children's education. If these parents believe their children are being shortchanged in the classroom, they are likely to advocate vigorously for their children's educational needs.

Developmental Changes

As children mature, their beliefs about effort and ability, success and failure, also change. Developmental changes that occur on cognitive, social, and emotional fronts as children age also alter their perceptions of themselves and their beliefs about what is necessary to preserve their sense of self-worth. What was relatively unimportant during one developmental stage may loom large in the next. Just as children's physical bodies undergo transformation as they develop, new levels of cognitive and emotional awareness also unfold within them. For example, Ames points out that

> Young children tend to have an optimistic view of their ability, high expectations for success, and a sort of resilience after failure. Moreover, young children tend to equate effort with ability. To them, hard workers are smart and smart children work hard. As children progress through school, their perceptions of their ability decrease and tend to reflect the teacher's evaluation of their ability. Older children's self-evaluations are more responsive to failure or negative feedback, meaning they are more likely to adjust their expectations downward after failing. Older children also develop a more differentiated view of effort and ability. While effort can increase the chance for success, ability sets the boundaries of what one's effort can achieve. Effort new becomes the "double-edged sword." Trying hard and failing threatens one's self-concept of ability.

If teachers are aware of how developmental changes may influence students' responses to learning situations, they will be able to structure more effective learning activities. They will also be better equipped to interpret and respond to, and work at reversing, maladaptive motivational patterns that have taken root in discouraged students.

As children develop, their perception of ability changes. "Studies find consistently the children's expectations for success at academic performance remain high, often unrealistically high, until about the second or third grade, and continue to decrease, on the average, throughout the elementary grades," states Deborah Stipek (1984). In young children's minds, there is not a clear delineation between effort and success. Young children tend to equate learning with ability, and since all young children are able to learn, they feel competent. Despite repeated failure at a task, young children tend to maintain a sense of optimism about their ability to succeed at the task in future attempts.

When they begin school, children's sense of ability gradually undergoes transformation. They come to think of ability as "being more able than others" and also subscribe to the notion that "success is more impressive when few succeed" (John Nicholls 1984). Their "optimism and readiness to try despite failure gradually diminishes with age" as their concept of ability changes (Nicholls).

Although students of all ages are concerned with preserving their sense of self-worth in the midst of learning situations, the methods older students employ to "save face" often differ from those embraced by younger students. Because some of the strategies used by older students are less straightforward, in many cases teachers may not recognize a student's attempt to maintain a sense of self-worth for what it is.

At first glance, some behaviors older students resort to when their self-concept of ability is threatened may appear to be propelled by a self-defeating motive. However, it is important for teachers to recognize that students engaging in such behaviors are trying desperately to minimize potential damage to their self-esteem and self-concept of ability.

Although strategies such as "not trying, procrastination, false effort, and even the denial of effort" in fact increase the likelihood of task failure, Ames (1990) contends that students who resort to such strategies are actually attempting to avoid some of the negative "fallout" of anticipated failure. She explains that "what these behaviors accomplish is reducing the negative implications of failure" by divorcing failure from effort. If they feel destined to fail, older students may prefer to fail at a task because of not putting forth sufficient effort than to exert considerable effort and still fail. From the student's perspective, if he fails without seriously investing himself in a task, he has achieved "failure with honor" because the failure experience cannot be attributed to lack of ability (Ames 1990).

Self-Perceptions of Ability and Competence

Children's views of themselves have powerful implications for their motivation to learn. Whether they see themselves as "origins" or "pawns" (Richard deCharms 1976), as able or helpless, as high or low in ability and competence, influences how they cope with learning situations. Based on messages they receive from outside sources, such as their parents, teachers, and peers, children gradually come to think of themselves as generally capable or incapable, competent or incompetent. This general sense of one's ability, sometimes called *self-concept of ability*, "has significant consequences for student achievement behavior" and for the way students respond to challenges and tasks that are set before them (Ames).

Especially after they enter the often competitive world of school, students begin making judgments about their sense of competence. Internally, they size up learning situations and decide whether it is likely or unlikely that they will be able to succeed at a given task. In addition to the nature of the task itself, students' self-perceptions of ability influence their assessment. Those who possess a strong sense of competence will be more apt to initiate and maintain involvement in activities, and, in doing so, will challenge and enhance their actual ability.

It is important to note that although a child's self-concept of ability may be distorted and based on erroneous input, this does not nullify its influence. For example, one student who had an SAT score in the 98th percentile mistakenly thought this meant he had an IQ of 98. Because he thought his IQ was 98, he anticipated that college-level work would be difficult for him. Sure enough, he did indeed struggle during his first year at college. He was ready to drop out, convinced he could not do this caliber of work. It was only later, after he received an accurate understanding of his SAT score and learned his IQ was really about 140, that his college performance began to soar. Soon he began doing "A" work. His newfound knowledge helped him to achieve his actual, rather than his perceived, potential (Raffini).

Self-Worth and Effort

People need to experience themselves as valuable, as having significance and worth. We all struggle for both self-approval and the approval of others. Two terms frequently used to characterize how people think and feel about themselves are *self-concept* and *self-esteem*. Self-concept involves the collection of perceptions we possess about such things as our strengths, weaknesses, abilities, personality traits, and performance of roles, while our self-esteem is a product of how much relative importance we attach to each of these specific personal attributes and roles (Raffini).

For example, if a person considers himself sloppy, but being tidy is not a priority, his view of himself as sloppy (part of his self-concept) will not have a detrimental effect on his self-esteem. However, if he considers neatness a virtue yet perceives himself as sloppy, then his self-esteem will be adversely affected.

Until children start school, they do not usually occupy formal roles outside their immediate family. Once they enter the public school system, however, children's overall sense of self-esteem or self-worth becomes closely linked to "their self-concept of ability in school settings" (Ames). Early in their educational experience, children often discover that what seems to matter most to their teachers, parents, and even peers is how their performance and perceived ability stacks up against that of other students, not how much effort they put forth or how much they improve their skills and abilities. Before long, they begin to internalize the sometimes subtle, sometimes not so subtle message that "good students" are high achievers and "poor students" are low achievers.

Students use a variety of strategies to try to preserve their sense of competency and self-worth in the classroom. Martin Covington (1984) refers to the tendency to establish and maintain a positive self-image as the *self-worth motive*. Because academic ability is often perceived as integral to the preservation of self-worth, students consider it critical to be viewed by others as intellectually capable and competent.

Unfortunately, many schools define success as stellar academic performance. And intelligence itself is often conceptualized quite narrowly, referring only to students' logical-mathematical and linguistic abilities. Although all students covet success and strive to be seen as able, some students' talents may lie in areas that are not formally recognized or accorded equal value with what is traditionally defined as "intelligence." Howard Gardner and Joseph Walters (1993), who believe human beings possess multiple intelligences, assert that "an exclusive focus on linguistic and logical skills in formal schooling can shortchange individuals with skills in other intelligences." They emphasize that "nearly every cultural role requires several intelligences" and that it is therefore important "to consider individuals as a collection of aptitudes rather than as having a singular problem-solving faculty that can be measured directly through pencil-and-paper tests." When schools recognize a wider range of human talents as having equal value with what has traditionally been defined as "intelligence," a greater proportion of students are able to regard themselves as being capable and talented.

Some schools and classrooms are strongly oriented toward competition rather than cooperation, which can make it more difficult for some students to define themselves as competent. When undue emphasis is placed on relative academic ability rather than progress and improvement, less able students are more likely to resort to defensive or maladaptive strategies with the intent of avoiding failure or minimizing the negative meaning of failure. Although misguided, these tactics are intended as solutions to the challenge of keeping their self-image and sense of competence intact.

Superficially, many strategies students engage in to ward off failure or the psychological fallout of failure may seem inconsistent with the goal of maintaining a positive self-image. However, on closer inspection it is evident that behaviors such as procrastinating, cheating, avoiding tasks, and setting impossibly high goals for oneself are actually employed by students to protect their sense of self-worth. Although ultimately ineffective, these strategies temporarily reduce some of the unwanted ramifications of failure.

For example, when a student procrastinates and only ends up studying briefly right before an exam, others will not tend to cast doubt on his ability if he subsequently fails the test. And if he performs well on the test despite investing only minimal effort to prepare for it, others will probably view him as possessing considerable ability.

Another strategy to avoid failure or minimize its effects is nonparticipation, which can manifest itself in a number of forms: slouching in one's chair to avoid being called on, appearing to be too busy taking notes for the teacher to interrupt, being inattentive, and, in its most extreme form, dropping out. Cheating and setting impossibly high standards for oneself are other ultimately self-defeating strategies employed to preserve a sense of competence and self-worth.

In situations where students are required to participate but expect to fail, they often reduce the level of effort they put forth. Students reason that if they expend minimal effort, their subsequent failure will not be as damaging to their sense of self-worth and competence because the failure probably will not be chalked up to a lack of ability. When students fail, the shame they experience tends to be less if their level of effort was low than if their level of effort was high (Covington). This helps to explain why students may withhold effort in circumstances where it might be assumed they would exert extra effort in the quest to succeed.

Raffini asserts that students do not "choose ignorance over competence when they have an equal choice. Many students reject school because they find the academic practices in their classrooms threatening to their sense of self-worth."

Raffini views student apathy as a "rational, albeit self-defeating defense mechanism" students use to cope with educational practices that limit the number of students who can feel good about their academic performance in school. While a few students are labeled "above average," the majority fall into the "average" or "below-average" range.

When students rely heavily on maladaptive failure-avoiding strategies, the consequence "is a progressive deterioration of the individual's will to learn," states Covington. "Psychologically speaking, this involves a transformation in the person from being success-oriented to becoming failure-prone and then, ultimately, failure-accepting."

Causal Attributions

Causal attributions have to do with students' beliefs about why they perform well or poorly on school-related tasks. The causes to which students attribute their successes and failures are another piece of the complex puzzle of motivation. The four most common things to which students attribute their success are ability, effort, task difficulty, and luck (Bernard Weiner 1980, cited in Raffini). Which of these is perceived to be the cause will make a big difference in how students experience their successes.

As Raffini states, "When students attribute their successes to effort, they experience feelings of pride since effort is both internal and individually controllable." Similarly, if ability is viewed as the reason for their success, students will also experience a sense of pride and confidence, because the cause of their success is a stable characteristic that resides within them, something that can be relied on to help them with future challenges. On the other hand, if luck is seen as the reason for success, students will neither take credit for nor derive satisfaction from their success, since luck is something over which they have no control.

Students will also be robbed of a sense of pride and competence in their accomplishment if they achieve success on a task that is characterized as easy by the teacher or the student.

While success-oriented students tend to attribute their achievement to a combination of skill and effort and their failure to a lack of effort, what Covington terms "failure-accepting students" tend to view failure as a sign of lack of ability or skill, a reflection of personal inadequacy. Unfortunately, although these students perceive failure as a sign of inadequacy, they do not conversely conceptualize success as resulting from personal adequacy. Instead, its source is attributed to external sources, "factors such as luck, task ease or the generosity of a teacher" (Covington). Students in this category may actively shy away from success experiences because with success comes an implicit expectation that they should be able to duplicate the experience in the future. Students who view their success as externally based are not certain they can produce more successful experiences, since their success is seen as emanating from a source outside themselves.

Wlodkowski and Jaynes point out that each experience involving students' effort and ability is a building block that lays the foundation for their future learning experiences:

> Gaining confidence as a learner is a spiral in which one's effort and ability result in achievement and that achievement serves as the mental foundation for the next extension of effort and ability in learning. We do, and we believe we can do more. By not trying their best in learning, students deny themselves and their society the endowment of their gifts.

Meaning of the Task

Meaning and motivation are closely connected. As we all can attest from firsthand experience, "whether or not persons will invest themselves in a particular activity depends on what the activity means to them" (Martin Maehr 1984). If an individual considers an activity to be meaningful, it is more probable she will invest herself in it. People possess a "package of meanings" based on past experiences that they carry with them to each new situation (Maehr). How we view ourselves, in combination with our beliefs, values, and so forth, all play a role in determining how we respond to new situations.

In addition to our personal history of experiences, aspects of situations and tasks themselves also have an impact on the meaning individuals attach to them. As Maehr points out, students make different judgments about the worth of specific tasks and "place different values on school tasks quite apart from their ability to perform." Whether competition is built into a performance situation, for example, will have an effect on how students respond to it. The element of competition does not seem to significantly impair the performance of students who view themselves as successful and competent, for competition may be seen as another opportunity to affirm their ability. On the other hand, students who do not consider themselves successful will tend to perform less well on the same task if it is organized in a competitive manner than if it is organized in a noncompetitive manner.

Autonomy

Like all human beings, students want to have some control over what activities they pursue and when and how they choose to engage in them. In environments where our tasks and activities are rigidly prescribed by others, our levels of responsibility and commitment often wane. As Raffini notes, this applies to teachers as well as students: "As teachers lose autonomy, they often feel less and less responsibility about meeting curricular requirements, they become cynical about teaching, they blame others for their cynical attitude, and they may even try to undermine the system if given an opportunity."

Although students may display their displeasure somewhat differently than teachers, a parallel pattern often emerges when they are denied a sense of self-determination. On the other hand, if students are given small choices on a regular basis, from such things as "whether to work on math before starting spelling, to where to place one's name on assignments," they will tend to respond positively to being able to make choices and ultimately become skilled at being self-governing.

In addition to small choices, it is important for teachers to give students significant and meaningful choices. By teaching students goal-setting skills and allowing them to map out some short-term learning goals for themselves, teachers can do much to foster students' sense of autonomy and self-determination (Raffini).

Relatedness and Belonging

Although the primary mission of schooling is frequently identified as that of acquiring academic skills and knowledge, there is no getting around the fact that school is a social as well as an intellectual experience. If students feel socially isolated or rejected by their peers, they will not enjoy their school experience. Attending school will be drudgery, no matter what lengths teachers go to make the material interesting and stimulating. And when students feel out of place in the classroom, their motivation to learn will suffer.

Whether students find a place in the group and feel "at home" in the classroom is influenced by classroom climate. "The classroom, under the leadership of the teacher, can either provide support and approval for all of its members or it can become an arena for constant competitiveness that builds a crystallized dichotomy of acceptance and rejection," states Raffini. By emphasizing cooperation rather than competition and assisting students who are less socially skilled, teachers can promote students' motivation to learn.

Conclusion

Even this cursory review of some factors that affect student motivation reveals it to be a complex subject with its own specialized vocabulary. As a means of summarizing some of the key concepts about motivation discussed in this chapter, table 1 offers brief explanations of several prominent terms.

While it is important for educators to appreciate the range of factors that can influence students' motivational orientations, awareness of theory is not sufficient to create change in the classroom. Theory needs to be translated into practice. However, instead of immediately moving on to classroom and school practices that may promote motiva-

TABLE 1

Terms Related to Motivation

Terms	Meaning
Intrinsic orientation	Learning is its own reward. It is undertaken for the knowledge, enjoyment, and sense of accomplishment it provides.
Extrinsic orientation	Learning is the means to obtain some other reward external to itself, such as a grade, a sticker, or a place on the honor roll.
Mastery goals	Students pursue learning in an attempt to develop new skills or gain mastery of the subject matter. Motivation to succeed springs from within, and students believe that effort leads to mastery.
Performance goals	Students pursue learning to bolster their self-worth and to be seen by themselves and others as competent.
Motivation to learn	Students find value in education and are willing to put forth effort to learn, even when it is not fun or pleasurable to do so.
Causal attributions	Most students attribute their success to one of four things: ability, effort, task difficulty, or luck. Students experience their successes differently depending on what they believe caused their success.

tion, the following chapter focuses on two central factors that profoundly affect students' attitudes toward school and desire to invest themselves in learning—caring and high expectations.

2

CARING AND HIGH EXPECTATIONS: CORNERSTONES OF MOTIVATION

When student motivation lags, teachers are tempted to seek a "quick fix" to remedy the problem. Articles abound that list a variety of gimmicks and strategies purported to be able to miraculously breathe life back into lifeless students. Although there are curricular strategies that can either encourage or discourage student motivation and engagement, enduring increases in student motivation are not likely to occur as a result of superficial changes, just as a troubled marriage will not be restored to health as a result of one partner buying flowers or a box of candy for the other.

In a marriage, the way the two partners interact and the expectations they have for one another are central to whether the relationship is experienced as meaningful, rewarding, and satisfying. Although flowers or some other token can be an outward expression of love and caring, in the context of a troubled marriage such a gesture may be an attempt to avoid engaging in, or to bypass, necessary substantive changes at a relationship level.

Although the analogy is an imperfect one, both teachers and students and husbands and wives are engaged in a relationship, and in teacher-student interactions as well as in husband-wife interactions how the parties feel within the context of the relationship influences—for better or for worse—their behaviors, actions, and attitudes. In addition to the nature and content of instruction, the affective climate and the overt and covert expectations that are present have a bearing on students' level of engagement in learning. And while it may be tempting for teachers to rush to "fix" flagging motivation by offering students a variety of instructional "bells and whistles," a shift may first need to take place in the way teachers interact with students and in the expectations that they hold for them.

A Sense of Caring and Connection

Caring may be thought of as the foundational soil that enriches students' educational experience, allowing them to feel connected to the school in much the same way a plant is rooted in and derives nutrition from the soil. Just as soil is vital to a plant, when students are aware of and feel supported by a sense of caring in the school environment, they have a solid, secure base from which to grow and take healthy risks emotionally, socially, and academically.

Students' feelings and attitudes about school are strongly linked to teachers. Whether they have positive or negative associations with school is primarily based on and directly related to their experience with teachers. As the report *Getting By: What American Teenagers Really Think About Their Schools* (Jean Johnson and Steve Farkas 1997) notes,

> The source of learning and achievement for... youngsters is the human being at the center of the learning process—the classroom teacher. Higher standards, more effective teaching techniques, better accountability, clearer goals—all may be necessary, but they are not likely to be sufficient. If students have teachers who care about them, expect much from them, and communicate a love of knowledge, the students will respond in kind. But all too often, the teens say, teachers appear to be uninterested, unwilling to challenge, and indifferent to the subjects they teach.

Unfortunately, teachers do not generally receive formal training about how to connect with students and understand their perspective. Because of this, they may fail to recognize that how they relate to students affects students' motivation to learn. Anne Wescott Dodd (1995), a former secondary school teacher, candidly recounts:

> When I was a first-year teacher, I was concerned with survival. My attempts to control students led to many power struggles from which both the students and I

emerged discouraged or defeated. These feelings were not conducive to teaching or learning.

I wish someone had told me then that knowing my students was as important as knowing my subject. I didn't realize until much later that to motivate and engage students, teachers must create a classroom environment in which every student comes to believe, "I count, I care, and I can."

Dodd believes that by being more attentive to students' thoughts and feelings teachers will be in a better position to facilitate student motivation and engagement:

> What teachers need most to know about students is hidden; unless they develop a trusting relationship with their students, teachers will not have access to the knowledge they need either to solve classroom problems or to motivate students.... As teachers learn more about how students think and feel, they will be able to create classes where students have fun *because* they are engaged in learning in diverse, purposeful, and meaningful ways.

The way in which students experience school at an emotional level is not generally one of the first things that springs to mind when the problem of student motivation is being discussed. As Robert Chaskin and Mendley Rauner (1995) note, "The emotional needs of children are often left out of discussions about how to improve student performance. Yet... caring interactions between teachers, students, and parents often make the difference between positive school experiences and frustration or alienation." Similarly, R. C. Vito, W. Crichlow, and L. Johnson (1989) underscore the centrality of students' feeling emotionally connected to their school environment. They state that "when students feel more connected to their schoolmates, teachers, and parents, and feel better about themselves, they will be more engaged in their learning than when they feel isolated or alienated from their surroundings."

In the relatively rare instances in which students have been asked what makes school appealing and meaningful to them, respondents consistently identify feeling cared about as a key element. For example, Patricia Wasley, Robert Hampel, and Richard Clark (1997) examined how school-reform efforts affect students. Their indepth study of 150 high school students from across the country sought to identify what changes matter most to students. Participants in the study repeatedly told the researchers that

> they responded better to adults who were concerned for their welfare. Caring teachers appeared more interested in youth and treated them more respectfully. Young people suggested that they worked harder for teachers who cared about them than those that seemed indifferent or cared only about their subject matter. (Wasley and others)

A fourth-grader participating in a study of caring by George Noblit, Dwight Rogers, and Brian McCadden (1995) expressed the connection between caring and motivation in a wrenchingly forthright way: "If a teacher doesn't care about you, it affects your mind. You feel like you're nobody, and it makes you want to drop out of school." Finally, a comment made by a high school student in a study by the Institute for Education in Transformation at Claremont Graduate School (Mary Poplin and Joseph Weeres 1992) also illustrates how deeply schools and teachers affect students, whether positively or negatively. When asked, "What is the problem of schooling?" the student replied, "This place hurts my spirit."

The depth of emotion conveyed in these students' statements underscores the significance of schools in students' lives. The message is unequivocal—it is not enough for teachers to possess strong instructional skills. Although teachers may have a comprehensive understanding of their subject matter and present the curriculum in a competent manner, if students do not feel a sense of caring from and rapport with their teachers, they are less likely to put forth maximum effort to learn.

Clearly, education consists of more than test scores and academic achievement, but even the goal of academic excellence will be compromised if feeling cared about is not an integral part of students' school experience. As Nel Noddings (1995) states, "We should want more from our educational efforts than adequate academic achievement... [but] we will not achieve even that meager success unless our children believe that they themselves are cared for and learn to care for others."

How Caring Can Be Conveyed in the School Setting

If the affective realm of students' school experience is related to student motivation and engagement, are there things teachers should be mindful of in their relationship with students? Are there specific characteristics that students associate with or view as evidence of caring by teachers?

Thankfully, research by Kris Bosworth (1995) sheds some light on questions such as these. Bosworth, who studied middle-schoolers' concepts of caring, identifies teachers as "the brokers of caring in schools." Teachers, Bosworth says,

> provide the bridge between the school and the individual. Understanding what adolescents see as caring behavior can facilitate communication between teachers and students and can help teachers model caring behavior. Hearing student voices can provide educators with a clearer understanding of approaches to enhance caring.

Bosworth interviewed middle-school students about their understanding of caring. About 90 percent of participants offered "complex, multidimensional definitions" and expressed a rich understanding of the concept. When asked about caring in a broad sense, students could clearly articulate what constituted caring interactions and provide examples of types of behaviors that might be manifestations of caring. *Helping* was the aspect of caring that emerged most frequently in students' discussions of the concept. Many students perceived of caring as embedded in ongoing *relationships*. Students also identified *values* such as kindness, respect, and faithfulness as being tied to and reflective of caring. The other commonly mentioned theme that emerged in young people's responses was *activities* that gave evidence of caring, such as spending time with another person.

When asked specifically "what they would see in a caring classroom," students showed they had clear notions about how caring might be manifested in the school environment. For example, one eighth-grade male student in Bosworth's study responded, "Everyone would be in their seats, doing work. The teacher would go around the room talking to everybody to see how they were doing [and] to answer questions. Sometimes she'd just say, 'Good job'." As Bosworth notes, the classroom situation envisioned by this student has many components to it. The hypothetical teacher "is involved with each student, meeting the needs of each student for specific help with an academic problem, or offering positive reinforcement and encouragement."

When all the responses were analyzed, characteristics of caring teachers identified by students in Bosworth's study were able to be sorted into three major categories— *classroom or teaching practices, nonclassroom activities,* and *personal characteristics.*

Teaching Practices (140 responses). The responses contained in this category not only included items such as helping with schoolwork, explaining work, and checking for understanding, but also personal traits such as valuing individuality, showing respect, encouraging students, and being tolerant.

Teachers' *willingness to help students with schoolwork* was the most frequently mentioned area within this category. Teacher assistance is, in and of itself, "a strong indicator that a teacher cares" (Bosworth).

Ways in which students saw teachers *valuing individuality* included inquiring about changes in students' behavior, recognizing different learning styles and speeds, and desiring to know students as unique human beings (Bosworth).

Showing respect, in the words of one student, entails having teachers who "treat you the way you want to be treated." Students also said teachers who show respect to them don't yell, and the teachers give them reprimands in private whenever possible.

Teachers demonstrated *tolerance*, according to the students interviewed, by providing opportunities for students to make up work they had missed or improve their behavior. They refrained from ridiculing students if they gave a wrong answer. However tolerance was not equated with low expectations or being lax. One seventh-grade student, for example, described her vision of a tolerant teacher as somebody who no matter what the student is, what their past was, would start off with a clean slate, just come in, make them feel good about themselves saying, "You're going to be one of my best students, and you will succeed in this class." Making them know from the start that they can do it.

Students, Bosworth found, also perceived caring teachers to be skilled at *explaining work* and, when appropriate, demonstrating how to proceed. Such teachers provide students with sufficient direction and guidance when making assignments.

Another way teachers can demonstrate caring, said the students, is checking to *make sure that students understand* what they are trying to convey. Students appreciate teachers who seek them out when they need additional clarification or explanation and provide them with the necessary supplemental assistance.

Offering students encouragement and helping them reach their full potential are other signs of caring cited by students in Bosworth's study. Some students explicitly stated that encouragement entails teachers' having and maintaining high standards and expectations for them rather than accepting poor quality work or low performance. One sixth-grader, for example, considered his teacher caring and encouraging because, "When you get bad grades, she says, 'You can do better than this'."

Nonclassroom Activities (81 responses). This category consists of things teachers do that fall outside the scope of their teaching responsibilities. Bosworth classified student responses into three subareas—*helping with personal problems, providing guidance,* and *going the extra mile.*

Responses in *helping with personal problems* included listening to students' concerns about difficulties they were experiencing at home or with peers and perhaps engaging in problem-solving with them.

Providing guidance involves goal-setting, advice-giving, and correction. Although one might assume that students would construe some of these behaviors as uncaring because they entail such things as teachers' contacting students' parents if they are disruptive, students seemed to comprehend that teachers had their best interest at heart in such situations, Bosworth reports. For example, one seventh-grade student in the study remarked, "A caring teacher doesn't let students get by with everything," and an eighth-grader said, "Sometimes they can be a little rough or angry with us when trying to look out for our well-being."

Going the extra mile included teachers' willingness to stay after school to help students with their work or talk with them about their problems. It also encompassed such things as attending athletic games or other school-sponsored functions. One student, for example, said the following about his teacher: "She is always available when we need help," and another stated, "She comes to every sport I play" (Bosworth).

Personal Attributes (48 responses). Responses in this category fell into four subgroups: *being nice or polite, liking to help students, being success-oriented,* and *being involved.* Within the *being nice or polite* subgroup, students spoke of teachers who smiled a lot and those who were not rude or mean.

Liking to help involved students' sense of teachers' availability and interest in helping them. Students' comments in this subarea included references to teachers' "devotion" and "effort."

Under the heading *being success-oriented*, students commented about teachers' belief in students' abilities and desire to see students succeed.

Subsumed under *being involved* were comments about teachers' "liking kids," being friends as well as teachers to students, and setting a good example. Students also used the word "involved" to describe caring teachers.

Missed Opportunities

In two schools studied by Bosworth, observers classified the majority of teacher-student interactions as neutral, neither overtly caring nor uncaring. Teachers were characterized as "clearly in charge" during instructional time, which emphasized lecture, silent seatwork, and other traditional teaching formats that don't facilitate caring interactions. Both schools were also under pressure to increase standardized test scores, which may have affected teachers' ways of working with students. That is, they may have focused so heavily on teaching "to the test" using traditional teaching strategies that they had little time left over for more personal contact with students.

Even given the structured nature of the school day, however, Bosworth found evidence of missed opportunities for demonstrating caring.

> We observed too many classes in which teachers rarely smiled, said anything positive to a student, or used a student's name other than for a reprimand. Changes in these behaviors might go a long way toward promoting caring and need not detract from the pursuit of academic goals. In a number of classes, students would seek help with a lesson or assignment only from the teacher. Often students had to wait their turn for the teacher to have time to answer their questions. Because the adolescents in this study identified helping as a key component of caring, schools that wish to provide opportunities for adolescents to demonstrate caring work to expand the pool of people who can help with schoolwork. (Bosworth)

If the schools Bosworth studied are representative of schools generally, then teachers and other school staff may benefit from reflecting on their daily contact with students and trying to objectively assess the extent to which missed opportunities have occurred. Such a review may raise teachers' awareness of how acts that may take only a matter of seconds, such as smiling at students while walking down the hall or greeting them by name, can positively affect the emotional and social climate within which learning takes place.

Indeed, when teachers are determined to display genuine caring to students because they consider it integral to education, Noblit, Rogers, and McCadden found they are able to do so despite the barrier created by the "technical rationality of schools" and the bureaucratic organizational structure typical of most schools.

When Noblit and colleagues studied Pam and Martha, two highly effective teachers at an inner-city elementary school, they found that although the teachers had very different teaching styles, both agreed on the importance of caring. It was woven into the relationships they formed with each of their students. It was the centerpiece within which both learning and discipline were embedded. As Noblit and colleagues note, the students in these teachers' classrooms "seemed to want to learn and to be orderly for the sake of their relationships with their teachers and classmates rather than to avoid punishment."

The climate created by a caring teacher can help to develop in students a desire to learn and act appropriately instead of a feeling of being compelled to do so because of a recognition that the teacher has power and authority over them. Students in caring classrooms are more likely to *want* to learn instead of feeling they *have* to learn, which has positive implications for student motivation and engagement.

The vignettes provided by Noblit and others illustrate how these teachers interacted with and assisted specific students in their classrooms depending on their individual needs. As the authors note,

> Every one of these stories is a little different because caring is expressed and received by each of the individuals involved in different ways.... What is evident in the... vignettes is how these teachers' expressions of care not only enhanced children's social skills and self-worth but also encouraged their academic development. Genuine caring is expressed by a teacher's attempt to assist students in reaching their full potential. No one can reach his or her full potential without social skills, a feeling of self-worth, strong academic and cognitive activities, and nurturance and support.

Although the two teachers studied by Noblit and colleagues showed their caring for students in different ways depending on students' individual needs, common threads were found in the comments made by the students at the school regarding what makes a good teacher. Students at the elementary school where Pam and Martha taught identified good teachers as those who helped them with their schoolwork but refrained from demeaning them for needing assistance.

Talking with students was another quality that set good teachers apart from mediocre teachers in the eyes of students at the elementary school where Pam and Martha taught. The children told the researchers that

> good teachers talked with them. Talk cannot be overemphasized, since it was through talk that children revealed their lives and teachers supported and nurtured them. Talk was reciprocal, requiring each to listen and hear as well as to speak. It was also through talk that teachers could help with schoolwork. Talk became the currency of caring; each opportunity to talk came to have a history and a future. (Noblit, Rogers, and McCadden)

In addition, Noblit and colleagues noticed that touch was another way in which teachers communicated caring to their students. The authors acknowledge that "touching is a politically sensitive issue today," and some schools and districts may discourage any touching by teachers for fear that it could be construed as having sexual intent and leave them open to potential lawsuits. But among the teachers and students Noblit and colleagues observed, touching was "a sign of relationship." Of course, school personnel need to be sensitive to possible adverse reactions by individual students to any form of touch and use good judgment in this area. Cultural differences concerning touch should also be taken into account. However, when expressed naturally and with sensitivity, touch can transmit a sense of caring.

As the material in this section indicates, caring is not something that lies at the periphery of teaching and learning. Rather, it should be the undercurrent that informs classroom climate and teachers' actions and interactions with students. When caring and respect are at the core of what occurs in classrooms, it is likely that increased motivation and engagement will be indirect outcomes.

More Students Speak Out

Kris Bosworth's study is one of surprisingly few in education that derived data directly from dialogue with students. Another study that stands out because it considers students' perspectives is *Voices from the Inside: A Report on Schooling from Inside the Classroom*, published by the Institute for Education in Transformation at the Claremont Graduate School (Poplin and Weeres). Recognizing the "tremendous gulf between life inside the schools and the perceptions of that life by academicians, policy makers, media, and community leaders," the year-long initial phase of the project was intended to discover the problems of schooling as perceived by the "voices from the inside"—students, teachers, parents, administrators, and other school personnel.

Over the course of a year, researchers interacted with the students, teachers, and parents at four Southern California schools selected to participate in the project. Ultimately, "24,000 pages of transcriptions, essays, drawings, journal entries and notes" and "18 hours of videotape and 80 hours of audiotape" were collected from people inside the schools.

When students at these schools were given the opportunity to articulate their views and identify the problems of schooling from their perspective, they often did so with eloquence and insight. To better understand student motivation, it is essential to see schooling through the eyes of students and to take the time to discover what's really important to them, what they like and don't like about school. To fail to listen to students' voices when attempting to unravel the mystery of student motivation is both arrogant and disrespectful. It seems somewhat akin to a physician proceeding to arbitrarily write a prescription for a patient who has not first been consulted about what's ailing him.

Relationships with Teachers. From the responses provided by students in this study, the one element that appears to most strongly influence whether school is a place they enjoy is the perceived presence or absence of caring. The nature of students' relationships with teachers is central to what makes school appealing or distasteful, inviting or uninviting. What students say they want is "authentic relationships where they are trusted, given responsibility, spoken to honestly and warmly, and treated with dignity and respect. They feel adults inside schools are too busy, don't understand or just don't care about them" (Poplin and Weeres).

Both teachers and students who participated in this project identified mutual caring as important. However, each group defined *caring* somewhat differently. Teachers thought their caring was evident in their professional commitment and devotion, and was communicated through such specific behaviors as "listening, consoling, and working hard."

Students defined caring somewhat more personally and more tangibly than did teachers. Students experienced teachers as caring when they directly stated that they cared, "when they laughed with them, trusted them, asked them or told them personal things, were honest, wrote them letters, called home to say nice things, touched them with pats, hugs, hand shakes or gave them the 'high five,' or otherwise recognized them as individuals" (Poplin and Weeres).

As Poplin and Weeres note, "The relationship between students and their teachers seems to dominate students' feelings about school." When students who were interviewed made positive comments about school, "they usually involve[d] reports of individuals who care, listen, understand, respect others and are honest, open and sensitive."

Students repeatedly "raised the issue of care" when asked about their school experience, stating that "what they liked best about school was when people, particularly teachers, cared about them or did special things for them." Conversely, students were vociferous about "being ignored, not being cared for, and receiving negative treatment."

A sampling of student responses contained in the report *Voices from the Inside* provides a window into students' experience of school as either caring or noncaring:

> "My teacher shows an honest concern about how we feel. He'll give us time to let our emotions out instead of just work, work, work." —high school student

> "My teacher just lectures and gives the assignment and then spends the rest of the class period behind the

desk. He has no regard for me as a person but just sees me as another student to be stereotyped." —high school student

"The perfect school would have the best teachers. Not necessarily the most educated but well-educated and fun. A curriculum that is challenging but also exciting and fun as well." —high school student

"My first period teacher seems so malevolent and shows no clemency towards us. We are supposed to have our hand shook every morning, this teacher does it with such an attitude like she doesn't want to. When I walk into my second period class, my teacher is there to meet you with a handshake and a smile which make you know it's going to be a good day. He knows your name which makes you feel good." —high school student

"Teachers should get to know their students a little better, not to where they bowl together but at least know if they have any brothers and sisters. I have found that if I know my teacher I feel more obliged to do the work so I don't disappoint them. Once my trust is gained I feel I should work for myself and also for the teacher." —high school student

"[Teachers] work with me through my problems in my studies and many of them can tell if I'm having difficulties in my life and sometimes they pull me aside for a pep talk." —high school student

"What I like about school is one of my teachers. It's the way she says things like 'dear' and 'sweetheart.' I love when people say things like that. I also like the way she talks to me like I am a human. My other teacher, I can't think of a thing I like. She looks over my shoulder when I am working. I can't stand it." —middle school student

"I think something should be done about teachers. They need to be reviewed more carefully because not all teachers are doing more good than harm and those who are, I believe are not getting enough recognition. I see that some teachers don't care, which is scary because of their power of influence. Teachers help create society. They should think about this." —high school student

Sound instructional content is undeniably important for schooling, but if it is not coupled with caring, teachers will not make much headway in encouraging students to want to learn. Students, just like the rest of us, need nurturing as well as knowledge. When there is a sufficient supply of caring in the school environment, instruction will be far more effective. The emotional lift that students obtain from feeling respected, cared for, valued will free them to concentrate their energies more clearly on the learning process. If students don't find respect in the classroom, many will choose to go outside the classroom to find it and will leave the learning process behind. In interacting with each student, teachers have an opportunity to convey caring and, with it (maybe *because* of it), content.

Maintaining High Expectations

As some of the students interviewed by Bosworth stated, caring is not antithetical to expecting the best from students. In fact, having high expectations is one way in which teachers can express caring. By believing in students' abilities and setting high standards for them, teachers are affirming students' potential. As Joan Lipsitz (1995) states,

> We do not have to choose between accountability on the one hand and caring school communities on the other. The issue is not whether we uphold expectations for our children, but what those expectations will be, how they will be expressed and implemented, and whose shared responsibility it will be to make sure that they are achieved. For instance, we are not being respectful or caring when we fail to teach children to read, compute, and write; nor are we respectful or caring when we hold differential expectations for children because of their race, gender, or economic status.

If students are allowed to perform at a minimum level and teachers are willing to accept low-quality work, students are likely to be less motivated and have less confidence in their own ability to perform challenging work.

Although some may assume that students accept or even relish lax teachers with low standards, ultimately students respect teachers more when they believe enough in them to demand more, both academically and behaviorally. In a recent national survey of over 1,300 high school students (Jean Johnson and Steve Farkas with Ali Bers 1997), teens were asked on questionnaires and through focus-group discussions what they think of and want from their schools. Teens' responses concerning what they want were clustered in three main areas:

• *A yearning for order.* They complained about lax instructors and unenforced rules. "Many feel insulted at the minimal demands placed upon them. They state unequivocally they would work harder if more were expected of them."

• *A yearning for structure.* They expressed a desire for "closer monitoring and watchfulness from teachers." In addition, "very significant numbers of respondents wanted after-school classes for youngsters who are failing."

• *A yearning for moral authority.* Although teens acknowledged cheating was commonplace, they indicated they wanted schools to teach "ethical values such as honesty and hard work."

Additional evidence of students' desire for challenging work and high expectations comes from a study conducted by Paulette Wasserstein (1995). When 200 seventh- and eighth-graders at Campus Middle School in Englewood, Colorado, were surveyed about their most memorable schoolwork, "again and again, students equated hard work with success and satisfaction" (Wasserstein). Survey responses given by the students led Wasserstein to the following conclusions:

1. Students of different abilities and backgrounds crave doing important work. All students benefit from opportunities to explore ideas for their own sake, and all students need to see the link between routine drill-and-practice and more complex work.

2. Passive learning is not engaging. For students to sense that their work is important, they need to tinker with real-world problems, and they need opportunities to construct knowledge.

3. Hard work does not turn students away, but busywork destroys them. Though all students must learn

the basics in order to move forward, the basics should not be an end in themselves but a means to an end.
4. Every student deserves the opportunity to be reflective and self-monitoring. Teachers can nurture a strong self-image by allowing students to develop an internal locus of control, aware of their strengths and weaknesses.
5. Self-esteem is enhanced when we accomplish something we thought impossible, something beyond us.

As Diane Ravitch (1995) succinctly puts it, "If more is expected of children, they will stretch to meet those expectations."

Student participants in a study of school reform conducted by Wasley, Hampel, and Clark also emphasized the importance of the complementary elements of caring and high expectations. At the same time students had a need to feel caring from teachers,

> it was critically important for young people to feel pushed, to feel that their teachers believed in their capabilities—sometimes more than the kids did themselves. They responded when their teachers were clear that students could do difficult work but that it would simply take effort and time. Students resented teachers who implied some work might be too difficult for them; they felt patronized, and it affected their self-esteem.

It is these two qualities in combination that facilitate change and that interact synergistically. As Wasley and colleagues note, "A school with *high expectations* for serious academic work from all students gets better performance of those expectations when *caring* for students gets equal attention" [Emphasis in original]. Conversely, "prominent scholars who have written about caring suggest that high expectations are part of caring—that teachers cannot be caring without expecting a good deal from their students" (Wasley and others).

Ms. Murray, a teacher in one of the five high schools studied by Wasley and colleagues, notes, "Just being a nice guy, making life easy, giving them a way out, that's not what's best for our kids.... Caring has to go both ways. Set strong goals and expect them to live up to those goals as you encourage and nurture them."

Steinberg asserts that student engagement is directly—not inversely—related to teachers' expectations. That is, when expectations are high, the level of student engagement rises to meet them. Conversely, when demands are minimal, engagement drops. According to Steinberg, for the most part student "disengagement is not a reaction to too much pressure or to classes that are too difficult, but a response to having too little demanded of them and to the absence of any consequences for failing to meet even these minimal demands."

However, Steinberg also acknowledges that student disengagement and low teacher expectations tend to function in a circular fashion, each exacerbating the other. He acknowledges that while it may be "tempting to. . . fault schools for having low standards and minimal expectations, and to see these factors as the causes of low student engagement and poor achievement," this is only part of the picture.

Steinberg contends that "the minimal standards and low expectations characteristic of most schools developed partly in response to low student engagement" and that each element feeds the other. That is, "students disengage from school, school demands less from disengaged students, students disengage further when little is demanded of them, and so on."

Teachers, aware of the bidirectional dynamics, can assess their own classroom situation, and, if necessary, take steps to restore appropriate expectations. Doing so will, in the long run, better serve students and ultimately raise their level of engagement and motivation.

This nation's parents and educators, Steinberg asserts, must instill in young people the belief that if they work hard in school, they will succeed.

> If there is a lesson we can learn from Japanese educators, it is not to be found by studying the ways in which they structure their school year, train their teachers, or organize their classroom activities. What we ought to

borrow from the Japanese—and communicate to every student and parent in this country—is the belief that success in school comes from hard work, not native intelligence, and that all children, if they are given instruction that is not only supportive, but appropriately demanding, can learn what they need to know to be educated and competent members of society. (Steinberg)

Conclusion

In sum, both caring and high expectations are essential elements that must be present in schools seeking to increase student motivation. When students sense they are sincerely cared about and know their teachers believe in their ability to succeed, the stage has been set for students to want to reach their full potential.

3

PERSPECTIVES OF PRACTITIONERS

Although students may not be aware of it, they derive many of their ideas about the purposes of learning from their teachers. And what students come to believe about learning, of course, has an impact on their motivation to learn. Most teachers do not stand before students and expound on their own philosophy of learning and achievement, but the way they structure their classrooms and respond to students reveals a great deal about the underlying assumptions they hold about learning and achievement. As Martin Maehr and Carol Midgley (1991) note, "Current research has suggested that students perceive classrooms as defining the purpose of learning in differing ways and that these perceptions influence the goals that students themselves adopt, thereby influencing their motivation and learning."

Teachers, to function successfully, must have some notion about what factors influence or promote student motivation. Either consciously or unconsciously, the way teachers function in the classroom is informed by their beliefs and assumptions about the purposes of learning and about what stimulates students' interest in learning. Curricular content and classroom culture are largely the outgrowth of teachers' beliefs about teaching and learning. Whether their gaze encounters predominately interested and engaged faces or blank, bored expressions, teachers continually confront the issue of student motivation during their daily contact with students.

Because they possess a rich reservoir of experience gained through interaction with students in the "real world" of the classroom, teachers are in a unique position to comment on the issue of student motivation. To give voice to practitioners, this chapter offers insights gleaned from interviews with an elementary school teacher, a secondary school teacher, and a principal of an elementary magnet school.*

Ted Nussbaum
Whiteaker Elementary School, Eugene, Oregon

Ted Nussbaum is an elementary school teacher whose ideas about student motivation rose from his experience "in the trenches." Nussbaum is currently on leave from the Eugene (Oregon) School District, where he taught at Whiteaker Elementary, a school with one of the largest populations of at-risk students in the state. His most recent experience at Whiteaker was in a first/second grade combination classroom. Nussbaum pinpointed many elements that enrich students' involvement and engagement in the classroom and school community.

Enthusiasm and Excitement

"One thing I get excited about is to see kids learning and I let them know I'm excited about it. I don't hide my excitement when kids are catching on. I tell the kids, 'There's always more things to learn and my goal is to teach you to be excited learners'." Teachers, he said, must find ways to feed their own sense of enthusiasm and excitement, because their attitudes about teaching and learning trickle down to their students.

High Expectations

Nussbaum is a firm believer in setting high goals for all students. He tries to communicate to students that "it is my expectation that you are going to accomplish the goals I set before you." Nussbaum contends that "when you have high goals, the kids tend to do better." On the other hand,

---

*In slightly altered form, the material in this chapter was originally published in *Motivating Today's Students* (Lumsden 1996).

the kids will often adjust their performance downward to meet your low expectations.

Choice

Nussbaum goes out of his way to let kids exercise choice in the classroom. For example, when handing out math worksheets, he tells students they can choose to work either all the even-numbered problems or all the odd-numbered problems. Then he says, "If you are a really hard worker, you can go back and do the other half of the problems." When he uses this approach, "changing it into a challenge instead of a command," about 90 percent of the students usually opt to do the other half of the problems, thereby identifying themselves as "really hard workers."

Responsibility

Although students are motivated by the opportunity to exercise choice, Nussbaum balances this freedom by emphasizing responsibility as well. "When they have responsibility, it's amazing how much more motivated they are." Nussbaum selects a student for the day, and that individual has the responsibility of taking the attendance form to the office and being line leader.

Kids come to enjoy a responsibility such as holding the classroom door open for their classmates because Nussbaum presents it as a privilege, a respectful act, rather than a burden.

Emphasizing the Positive

"When I grade papers, I put how many problems a student got right out of the total number possible, for example, 43 out of 50, instead of minus 7. And then when students have accomplished their goal by going back and correcting the problems they initially got wrong, I put an OK and then put 50 out of 50 on their paper. There's something about them knowing they've accomplished everything they need to accomplish that really boosts their morale. If a student complains, 'Man, I missed 7!' I try to turn it around and say, '43 out of 50, that's a lot; you did a good job!' "

Cooperative Learning

Students need to feel a sense of responsibility and accountability toward their peers rather than just toward the teacher, he said. This can be facilitated through cooperative learning experiences.

However teachers need to exercise care and attend to many factors when forming groups. Nussbaum sees to it that the slightly more mature second-graders in his first/second-grade classroom are fairly evenly dispersed among the groups he composes, attempts to place a student with leadership ability in each group, and so forth.

Nussbaum believes that when students work together they tend to motivate one another to accomplish the group goal. Each student has an individual challenge or a task to perform, without which the group goal cannot be achieved.

Encouragement

When a student is having an awful day, Nussbaum looks for one small act performed by the student that is positive rather than negative in nature. For example, if a student was disrupting the class and then spontaneously stopped and picked up papers on the floor by his table, Nussbaum would give him a "Gotcha Award" to recognize the thoughtful act. Being acknowledged for doing a small positive act in the midst of a "rotten day" is sometimes enough to help students alter their attitude and get back on track.

Nussbaum is demonstrative in affirming students. He sings to students on their birthday, leads class cheers, and puts up charts that record when they lose their teeth. A cheer is done for the Kid for the Day, and special cheers are given to class members who may be discouraged or confronting particularly difficult life circumstances.

"Sometimes if a kid has had a rough day or a rough night, I'll say, 'Is there anybody here who needs us to applaud for you? Come on up front,' and they come up and we just clap for them. If you've ever had that done for you, it may feel a little awkward but it reaffirms that they are an important person and that they are enjoyed and loved by the people in the class."

"Marbles in the jar" is another approach used by Nussbaum to affirm students. When the class as a whole is working quietly and focusing on what is supposed to be done, he drops a marble in a glass baby food jar. "Basically I've trained the kids to know that when they hear the marble dropping into the jar, they should keep on working but recognize that the sound of the dropping marble is the equivalent of a pat on the back." When the jar is full of marbles, the class is entitled to a special activity. Typically class members vote on what to do—watch a movie with popcorn, have free time in the classroom, play a group game, or pursue some other mutually selected option.

Discipline

For a classroom to function well, with students engaged, a teacher must handle disruptive behavior with skill. Nussbaum said it helps him to be prepared, that is, to have a sense of how he is going to intervene if a student gets off track behaviorally. "When a child does something that would normally make me angry, I turn it into an opportunity to teach that child," he said.

In a nutshell, concluded Nussbaum, "When you have fun yourself, the kids are going to have fun. When you are motivated yourself, they are going to become motivated."

Cindy Boyd
Abilene High School, Abilene, Texas

As part of an informal process she uses to evaluate and refine her teaching, Cindy Boyd periodically asks her students for feedback. One of the questions she poses is: "What have I done that has helped you the most?" Last year one student wrote, "You didn't teach me a thing! I had to learn to teach myself."

Although this student may have intended his comment as a criticism, Boyd received it as a high compliment. After reading it, she thought to herself, slightly amused, "Well, that's exactly what I meant to do!" Boyd speculated that this student was probably "so used to being spoon fed that he was real mad about having to learn to think" in her classroom.

A high school math teacher at Abilene High in Abilene, Texas, Boyd is an innovative educator with a teaching career that spans twenty-three years. She was selected from among 1,800 teachers as the Walt Disney / McDonald's National Mathematics Teacher of the Year for 1995. Among other professional honors, she has been a three-time recipient of the Texas Presidential Award.

Many have tried to lure her out of the classroom with lucrative job offers (some at triple her current salary), but Boyd has elected to remain in the classroom out of a deep-seated sense of mission and dedication. Her goal is to improve the teaching of mathematics, to share classroom innovation, and to give students a positive view of teaching and learning. Boyd characterizes her room as "a mathematical community where the students experience ownership of their learning and that of their partners as they strive to become life-long learners."

She is convinced that *"how* we teach is as important as *what* we teach." Guided by her passionately held convictions about teaching and learning, Boyd uses a variety of nontraditional formats in her largely self-created curriculum to bring to life a wide range of mathematical concepts and theorems in a classroom where her own sense of caring and enthusiasm are cornerstones. "It's got to be different right now to get their attention. The same old stuff isn't going to work. Worksheets and examples on the board—that just doesn't cut it."

She said, "My students have modeled 3-D shapes with Play-doh, folded paper to demonstrate theorems, fashioned geometric shapes with rubber bands on pads, built patterns with toothpicks, formed polyhedrons with straws, used computers and graphing calculators, graphed with colored magnets and cookie sheets, modeled algebraic equations with algebra tiles, and solidified ideas with popsicle sticks and wing nuts. My pupils sing and manipulate their way through concept after concept to what I feel is a better understanding of mathematics."

Describing the process she engages in to decide how to present material, Boyd said, "What I try to do is to look at a lesson, look at what the book has to offer, and ask myself, 'Do I really want to teach it this way?' And if I don't—and most of the time I don't—if I think I have a better idea, then I try to go from there."

Sometimes she starts out with a real-world application of a particular mathematical process. Whatever her particular approach, however, she actively involves the students rather than merely attempting to "download" information from herself to her students:

> Most of the time we go through a discovery process. I play the devil's advocate so they're kind of teaching me, explaining the concept to me. First we summarize our findings in our own words, we talk about the idea, about what we discovered, until it's pretty well crystallized. Then we go through it in a skit where it is further crystallized, and then in a song, where we play with it and have fun with it. And then we may follow that with a card game or a worksheet to give them some practice and increase their skill.

Boyd's relationship with her students and with her subject matter cannot be distilled down to a simple "formula" that can be duplicated in schools across the country. Much would be lost and cheapened in the translation process. However, the ten components mentioned below, all integral to Boyd's approach to teaching, may serve as a jumping off point and an inspiration for other educators who want to enliven their teaching and increase student motivation and engagement.

Atmosphere

Boyd strives to create "a physical and an emotional climate that encourages risk-taking and invites exploration." The physical appearance of her classroom probably more closely resembles a typical primary classroom rather than the traditionally bland secondary school classroom. Large honeycombed tissue apples, transparent globes, and models formed from coat hangers dangle from the ceiling. Manipulatives of all kinds line the shelves, offering an open invitation to students to "investigate, question, hypothesize, explore, and discover."

Brightly colored signs grace the walls, some reminding students of mathematical definitions, postulates, and theorems, others issuing challenges and conveying high expectations. For example, one sign reads, "I want to be the best teacher you've ever had. I expect you to be the best students I have ever had."

Boyd concentrates on creating an atmosphere characterized by trust, support, cooperation, and high expectations. She notes, "Concern that my students learn math is closely linked to a concern that my students have a healthy self-image. Students and I celebrate math daily. We talk about and laugh about mathematical relationships as we flex our mental muscles through concept development, problem-solving, and higher order thinking."

Activities

Boyd is not one to stand in the front of the classroom and drone on endlessly to a bunch of glassy-eyed pupils. She views students not as passive recipients of information but as active participants in the learning process. "I have always believed that good teaching actively involves students." Over the years, Boyd has learned that "activity-based, student-centered lessons pique and hold the interest of all students."

When planning lessons, she tries to develop ways of presenting the material through a variety of sensory modalities—visual, auditory, kinesthetic, and so forth—to reach the whole range of learning styles represented in her classroom and to solidify in students' minds the concept she is trying to convey. By essentially teaching the same thing in several different ways, she leaves students with a deeper, more comprehensive understanding of the material.

She supplements whole-class instruction with cooperative learning. When students work together in small groups or in pairs, they "help each other learn and think and reason" in a way that cannot be done during whole-class instruction.

Use of Auxiliary Items

"Almost any conceivable item can become an auxiliary item if it helps students to visualize the mathematics or to concretely represent a concept." One series of hands-on lessons involves Play-doh. For example, students form a cone, then use string to make two perpendicular slices and divide the cone into four congruent parts. This enables them to actually see the right triangle made of the height, slant height, and radius. Similar exercises with Play-doh help them more easily grasp mathematical concepts related to cubes, pyramids, and spheres.

Alternative Assessment

As Boyd notes, "Teaching differently requires testing differently!" Assessment, considered an integral part of the instructional process, is woven into the fabric of Boyd's courses. For example, two mathematical board games she developed serve as one alternative assessment tool that generates information about students' working knowledge of mathematical concepts.

Boyd's students also engage in self-evaluation when they make predictions and hypotheses about graphs and then use a graphing calculator to see if their expectations are borne out.

Anxiety Reduction

Boyd does her best to quell math anxiety by being sensitive to students' learning styles, giving assignments that have real-world applications, having students work collaboratively and use hands-on activities, showing students math can be fun, and, perhaps most important, facilitating firm understanding of mathematical concepts. When students are provided with ample opportunities to practice, and thereby solidify, what they are learning, they strengthen their working knowledge of mathematics, which "dispels worry and fear."

Attitude

Boyd poetically refers to attitude as "the paintbrush of the soul." She notes that "a positive attitude and a willingness to work can overcome almost any deficiency." She attempts to model not only an upbeat outlook but also such qualities as persistence, problem-solving, encouragement, and cooperation.

Applause

Boyd focuses on what her students are doing right and praises them for that. She also creates a climate where students become "genuinely excited by the success of their peers." And she believes peer-based positive feedback is perhaps the most meaningful and inspirational form of "applause" for students.

Applications to Everyday Life

Boyd shuns teaching math compartmentally; instead, she integrates it with science, music, language arts, social studies, and other disciplines, which helps students view mathematics as having greater relevance to their lives. "Cross-curricular emphasis gives new meaning to math concepts" and better equips students for life in the outside world.

Animated Assimilation, or Life-Long Learning

A central goal of Boyd's is to nurture in her students "a love of learning that will last for the rest of their lives!" She models enthusiasm for life and learning on a daily basis and maintains an attitude of inquiry and interest. In the aftermath of a close brush with death in 1985, Boyd came to the conclusion that she had been given a second chance at life "to make a difference in mathematics education by teaching students differently and by sharing my insights with my peer teachers and with students."

Association with Each Other and with the Subject Matter

Relationships are often overlooked in teachers' earnest quest to fill students with specific information. Learning does not occur in a vacuum, but in a context. When elements such as caring, support, creativity, and respect characterize the relational context, both among students themselves and between teachers and students, the process of learning is stimulated rather than stunted.

The most effective way to bring about change in education, believes Boyd, is for innovative teachers to remain in the system to make it better. She takes heart in knowing that some of her students will choose to become teachers who will teach differently as a result of being taught differently, and they, in turn, will inspire others, thereby passing the torch to yet another generation of learners.

Howard Pitler
L'Ouverture Computer Technology Magnet, Wichita, Kansas

The sign above his office door reads: "Principal Learner." It captures one central belief of Howard Pitler, principal of L'Ouverture Computer Technology Magnet: There's always more to learn. Conveying to students that learning is a never-ending, exciting quest underlies the efforts made by Pitler and the staff at L'Ouverture to keep students motivated and to continually expand their learning horizons.

Built in 1912 as an elementary school for black children and named for Toussaint L'Ouverture, a famous Hatian military leader who fought the French colonists in 1800, L'Ouverture is now a racially diverse elementary school in the Wichita, Kansas, inner city. The school has received many accolades. L'Ouverture won the Kansas Better Schools Award, was selected as an Outstanding Focus School by the Kansas Association of Elementary Principals, was named a "Models for Success School" by Computer Curriculum Corporation, was identified by *Redbook Magazine* as One of America's Best Schools in the category of "overall excellence," and is one of only twenty-five schools in North and South America to be named an Apple Distinguished Program.

The school has also been featured in *Education Week*, the *Harvard Education Journal*, and *People* magazine. And to top it off, Pitler was named Kansas Elementary Principal of the Year by the Kansas Association of Elementary Principals at its 1996 conference. He was also chosen as National Distinguished Principal for 1997-98.

As the person at the helm of this innovative, inspirational school, Pitler offered his perspective on what it takes to keep students interested and engaged in learning.

Authentic Tasks

The foremost step educators can take is to assign students "authentic tasks rather than made-up coursework." Pitler offered an up-to-the-minute example. "Two of my fifth-graders and I just got back into the building after going to the United Urban Ministry Food Bank. We were talking with them about developing a website for the organization so that they would have more visibility in the community and be able to draw on resources they don't currently have available. They bought the idea and now those two fifth-grade girls are back in their classroom designing the home page. [Earlier, students at L'Ouverture developed a website for the Wichita Symphony, which they maintain and update.] Monday morning they have to present their design to the executive director and the board of the Urban Ministry."

As part of the project, the two fifth-grade students will also evaluate and rewrite some of the text for brochures produced by the Urban Ministry.

Pitler provided another example of an "authentic" task. He arranged for a student to interview a candidate for Congress who was scheduled to visit the school. The interview was then broadcast on the live daily TV show that is produced at L'Ouverture.

Another student interviewed the governor of Kansas. When Pitler approached the student he had in mind to conduct the interview, she took the assignment in stride. "She didn't say, 'I can't do that!' or 'You've got to be kidding!' She wasn't intimidated by interviewing the governor or by doing it in front of 400 people."

The process of preparing for and conducting interviews helps students strengthen their research skills and their written and oral communication skills. At the same time, experiences like this help to bolster students' confidence.

Genuine Caring

Authentic assignments build students' commitment to the work they are asked to complete. The second thing the school staff can do to keep kids motivated is to genuinely and openly demonstrate their caring for students. At L'Ouverture, this message of caring is expressed directly, both verbally and through physical touch.

Although he expressed concern that this crucial element may sound "trite or trivial," Pitler said, "Simply put, we love our kids.

> We are a high touch environment; that's in our mission statement. We hug kids and when we talk to them we put a hand on their shoulder. We know them by name, we know their families by name, and we make sure that they know we truly care about them. It's much easier to motivate them when they actually think you like them.

Staff Quality and Camaraderie

L'Ouverture has "exceptionally good teachers who all care about the kids." Pitler noted that the teachers consistently go "above and beyond" the requirements of their positions, regularly attending school-related events for which they do not receive financial compensation. "That's what our folks are like," he said.

Staff members—who are "very close knit"—help one another remain motivated. For themselves as well as for their students, these teachers have "great expectations." If the level of performance of any single staff member starts to falter, others will typically surround them with support and assistance.

High Standards and Individualized Student Goals

At L'Ouverture, the assumption is that students will maximize their potential. As Pitler said, "We expect kids to perform—we don't see that as optional. Your job while you're here is to learn." Although high expectations are maintained, Pitler acknowledged that instruction must be tailored to a student's individual level of performance. Individualized educational plans (IEPs) are developed for *all* students, not just for those who receive special-education services. Each student's IEP identifies specific goals for performance based on the student's current level of functioning.

Pitler noted, "We've got second-graders who are reading at the seventh-grade level, so we work with them at that level. And we've got fifth-graders who are working at a third-grade level and we work with them at that level. But everybody needs to demonstrate growth, whether you are a gifted child who is five grades above grade level or you're a child working two grades below grade level."

Lifelong Learning

A teachable, aspiring spirit and an inquisitive mind are not qualities cultivated only in the students, however. Teachers do not put themselves up on a pedestal nor do they strive to be seen as omniscient. At L'Ouverture, learning is not bounded by formal roles and positions. "We all model the fact that there's no one in this building who can possibly know everything they need to know."

Teachers view students as resources, not as empty vessels awaiting knowledge to be imparted from on high. Most staff members feel comfortable asking students to help them fill in some of their own learning gaps. For example, teachers may call upon students to share their expertise in website design and construction.

Cooperative Learning and Teamwork

Collaboration is another hallmark of life at L'Ouverture, and one that motivates and energizes those who work together. Through their teamwork, kids come away with a greater appreciation of one another's strengths and talents. "What the kids learn," said Pitler, "is that even though some kids are real good in math and other kids are real good in language arts, everybody is real good in some area."

Everyone contributes to group efforts, regardless of their abilities. "A kid who is not necessarily the best student in the class is still going to be an active participant. And one responsibility of the team is to make sure that everybody comes along."

Pitler said, "I am watching a project outside my window right now where kids are working in small teams planting tulips in different plots of ground. The students will be tracking the arrival of spring on the computer. Classes all over the country are planting the same variety of tulips at the same time. They are going to be charted on a map when they start to bloom around the country. The students will watch the blooming pattern as it moves up from the equator, up to Canada."

In a typical classroom, students work together in different "centers." He said, "If we were to walk into the classroom, what you would see is five centers in operation, each having a different activity. Depending on the teacher, some signal is given about every twenty-five to thirty-five minutes, and kids will stop what they're doing, get up and move to a different center, and begin a new activity."

In addition to working together in small groups, students of different ages are also paired together through peer-to-peer tutoring, which is motivating for both parties involved. As part of their scope-and-sequence requirements, all fifth-graders are assigned to teach first-graders how to use Hypermedia and to help them develop a Hypermedia project. Similarly, fourth-graders work with third-graders on projects, and second- and third-graders are paired with residents of the senior center across the street. "Everybody has some kind of intergenerational peer to work with," said Pitler.

Student-Led Conferences

Started initially by two teachers at the school and then expanded the following year, this form of conferencing with parents is "another great motivator," well received by students and parents alike.

The student goes through a fairly rigid structure that has been worked out in advance. It takes two or three weeks for the student to prepare for the conference with their parents. During the process they share portfolios and provide demonstrations. They also share with their parents "what they perceive to be strengths and weaknesses in their own performance, what they see as areas where they need to improve."

Circulating around the room, Pitler has overheard students say to their parents, "I'm really pretty good at doing this and this, but there are some kids in class who are better than me in this. And some of my classmates tell me that when I do this in our groups, it really bothers them."

As he hears these types of comments coming from the students themselves, Pitler feels proud of students' ability to engage in self-evaluation and to accurately assess and reflect upon their own strengths and needs. At such times, he thinks to himself, "Well, we've won! When the kids can internalize that and say, 'Here's what I need to learn'—and we're talking about kindergartners and first-graders as well as fourth- and fifth-graders—we're doing something right." Indeed.

Conclusion

Being charged with educating the upcoming generation for the rapidly changing world of the future is an awesome responsibility. Teachers' own attitudes about learning and the way they relate to students combine to help shape whether students develop a "have to" or a "want to" attitude toward school and learning, whether they come to view learning as exciting or boring.

If teachers and school leaders are committed, creative, and passionate about what they do, students may begin to equate learning with inquiry and discovery. Ultimately, they may choose to become lifelong learners who value and pursue learning for its own sake.

4

CLASSROOM CONSIDERATIONS

It seems so obvious it hardly needs to be said: Classrooms are places where students and teachers come together for a purpose referred to as "education." Look closely at actual classrooms, however, and you will find that educators have radically different ideas about what this means. To a large extent, what transpires in specific classrooms is the reflection of individual teachers' and administrators' beliefs about what constitutes education and learning. There is significant variability in how educators define the mission of both the school and the classroom. What one may identify as a central governing principle, another may consider a relatively less important ingredient in the organization, management, and culture of schools and classrooms.

Every teacher, administrator, and support-staff member brings different strengths, experiences, personality traits, and beliefs to the school, as do all the students. The teacher and the students both contribute to the "feel" and functioning of specific classrooms. However, according to Raffini, in some respects the tenets subscribed to by teachers' beliefs are primary because it is these beliefs that

> determine how teachers structure teacher/student communication, establish norms for the classroom and select a style of leadership.... These beliefs can also strongly influence the classroom's goal orientation; some beliefs support the development of content mastery for all, while others tend to support the sorting and ranking of students so as to reward those who excel. The application of these beliefs is also represented by the structure and organization of the specific learning activities selected by the teacher. In summary, a teacher's beliefs regarding learners, learning, and teaching creates the overriding disposition of a

classroom's personality. The character and temperament of this personality are shaped by the teacher's leadership style and by the goal orientation he or she fosters in students.

While the uniqueness and individuality of schools, classrooms, teachers, and students should be cherished, the presence of certain elements at the classroom and school level can positively impact student motivation and attitudes toward learning.

To honestly approach the issue of student motivation and engagement, teachers and administrators must resist the temptation to adopt a "blame the student" mentality, thereby absolving themselves of the need for professional self-examination. Those who are willing to step back and objectively review their own professional practices and the attitudes and the beliefs on which they are based will be in a better position to work effectively with students and provide an environment in which motivation can flourish.

Two central elements that affect student motivation—caring and high expectations—were discussed in chapter 2. This chapter looks at several other classroom-level factors—ranging from a supportive classroom climate to instructional methods and the difficulty and variety of work teachers assign—that have the potential to affect student learning and motivation. Schoolwide strategies that may positively affect motivation and engagement are examined in the next chapter.

A Supportive, Respectful Climate

Students will shrink into silence and shy away from the risks inherent in learning if acceptance and security are not at the foundation of a classroom's psychological climate. As Brophy (1986) states, "Anxious or alienated students are unlikely to develop motivation to learn academic content." Conversely, if students experience the classroom as a supportive place where there is a sense of belonging and everyone is valued and respected, they will tend to participate more fully in the process of learning.

Although there are similarities between caring and support, and the two often go hand-in-hand, *support* has to do with providing an environment conducive to students achieving their full potential as well as taking an active role in helping them get there. Teachers who value all students equally and regard such things as students' effort, interest, reasoning skills, problem-solving strategies, and character as highly as their ability to spew out "correct" answers on cue are fostering a classroom climate that will help students retain their natural motivation to learn.

As mentioned earlier, it is a misconception to equate a caring and supportive environment with lower teacher expectations or lower student performance. Just because teachers create a supportive environment doesn't mean they are "pushovers" on the academic front. Classroom environments experienced as supportive by students are related to better—not worse—attitudes and outcomes. As Catherine Lewis and colleagues (1996) note,

> Students work harder, achieve more, and attribute more importance to schoolwork in classes in which they feel liked, accepted, and respected by the teacher and fellow students. Warm, supportive relationships also enable students to risk the new ideas and mistakes so critical to intellectual growth.

When students are confident that support and useful feedback will follow on the heels of their offering a "wrong" answer, they will be more prone to actively participate in and learn from what occurs in the classroom. When a foundation of support exists, inaccurate understanding and misapplication of skills or deductive reasoning errors can serve as the basis for productive class discussion and pave the way for deeper understanding and insight. For this type of analysis to succeed, however, teachers must first create a classroom environment in which all students feel safe and free from fear of ridicule or embarrassment. As Lewis and others note, "It is no coincidence that, to create an environment in which students can discuss classmates' incorrect solutions to math problems, Japanese teachers spend a great deal of time building friendships among children and a feeling of classroom unity."

A supportive environment "is not one that avoids criticism, challenge, or mistakes" (Lewis and others). Rather, it facilitates more substantive learning.

As Parker Palmer (in Lewis and others) points out,

> A learning space needs to be hospitable not to make learning painless but to make painful things possible... things like exposing ignorance, testing tentative hypotheses, challenging false or partial information, and mutual criticism of thought. [None of these] can happen in an atmosphere where people feel threatened and judged.

One study looked at teachers (Jere Brophy 1982, in Raffini) who were judged by their principals to be extremely skilled at assisting students who possessed deeply ingrained defeatist attitudes toward learning as a result of repeated failure experiences. This study found that "these highly competent teachers refused to cave in to these students by reducing expectations and treating them as if they were really unable to succeed." However, as Brophy (in Raffini) reports, they did more than merely raise the academic bar for these students. They also provided encouragement, support, and active assistance:

> These teachers reassure the students that they do have ability and that work given will not be too difficult for them. Then, the teachers help them to get started when they are discouraged or need some support, reinforce their progress.... In general, the emphasis is on encouragement and help rather than prodding through threat of punishment. Failure-syndrome students are not merely *told* that they can succeed, but *shown* convincingly that they can, and *helped* to do so. (Brophy, in Raffini)

Respect is also a key. Whether students feel they are being treated with "decency and fairness" has a lot to do with their commitment to learning (William Firestone and others 1990). Firestone and colleagues note that "there is a substantial association between students' commitment and their sense that they are treated with respect.... Students' sense that they are accepted by adults in the school does more than just bring them in, it motivates them to take the academic enterprise seriously."

Learning is not a straight, smooth, direct road to a destination. The journey is punctuated with wrong turns and dead ends, obstacles and challenges. Everyone wants to feel competent immediately, yet learning almost any new skill is a *process*. Fluency and competence take time and repeated practice to develop. And getting lost temporarily is often part of the journey. As Richard Strong, Harvey Silver, and Amy Robinson (1995) point out, "People who are highly creative... actually experience failure far more often than success."

Students—be they adults or children—need support when venturing into uncharted territory, where competence is still off in the distance, with several intervening hills. But if students are exposed to a narrow or superficial view of education, where mistakes are not viewed as an acceptable, even valuable, part of the process, the definition of learning they come to carry with them will be a distorted one. If they receive the message that getting the "right" answer supersedes everything else, and if process and character take a backseat to performance, much will be sacrificed. As Wlodkowski and Jaynes state:

> Today, many people seem to view the attainment of a hefty grade-point average and peak scores on the Scholastic Achievement Test as the ultimate indicators of being a successful student. We certainly think such accomplishments are noteworthy. Yet we are concerned that the current American obsession with such signs of achievement has reached a point of diminishing returns and harmful influence.
>
> Such gross emphasis on scores and grades as the most important aims and reflections of learning narrows the benefits of learning and pressures students to seek the most expedient means to external recognition of what they have learned. In short, it leads them on a steady path to joyless learning. In the throes of such a miserly vision, students have to work very hard to avoid becoming cynical about the higher purposes of a decent education.

Deemphasizing Competition

Motivation and learning goals can also be colored by the element of competition. Until recently, it was assumed that competition would motivate students and cause achievement to rise. However, recent research indicates otherwise. As Carole Ames and Russell Ames (1984) note, numerous studies have come to the same conclusion: that "competition leads to a number of debilitating motivational impacts."

A competitive classroom environment can be particularly problematic for those students whose academic performance does not compare favorably with that of their classmates. In a competitive environment, frequently the more these students struggle to "stay with the pack," the further they fall back, and the deeper they sink into the quagmire of discouragement. The sense that they don't measure up becomes magnified and this, in turn, further impairs the learning process. Although these students may be trying as hard or harder than other students, making progress, and mastering new skills, their achievements often receive scant recognition in classrooms where relative performance rather than individual progress is the yardstick by which students' academic prowess is measured.

As Judith Meece and Wendy McColskey (1997) note, "Research on motivation suggests that cooperative learning activities can have a positive influence on students' ability perceptions and motivational orientation." In highly competitive classrooms, students may consider their classmates adversaries instead of allies. Conversely, in classrooms where cooperation and interdependence are stressed—skills essential to success in the "real world"—it is easier for all students, instead of only the "cream of the crop," to feel good about their accomplishments. Collegial classrooms teach students to work together and appreciate the strengths and contributions of their peers. Classrooms that deemphasize competition are more conducive to students' concentrating on their individual progress and improvement. When the classroom structure downplays cross-student comparisons, students are more able to channel their energy into recognizing where they are, charting a course to where they want to be, and then moving in that direction.

The way teachers group students can affect the level of competition in a classroom. Forming heterogeneous instead of homogeneous groups of students can promote cooperation and interdependence. One "motivating" teacher in a study by Hermine Marshall (1987), for example, paired students with a high level of interest in science with those with a low interest in the subject, brought together students with a cross-section of skills when creating spelling groups, and always took into account both academic and social skills when making decisions about group composition. Some teachers intentionally bring together students with a variety of talents to work on a project where each individual's special strengths are required.

Meece and McColskey recommend keeping several factors in mind when forming cooperative learning groups, including the following:

- *Size*—groups with three to five students typically work best
- *Ability composition*—mixed-ability groups are most successful when the range of abilities among group members is not too extreme. Groups of similar-ability students should be avoided as much as possible because of the status hierarchy that is created by dividing students in such a manner.
- *Gender composition*—mixed-gender groups foster better relations between boys and girls, but girls tend to participate more actively in same-sex groups. A fairly even mix of boys and girls is necessary to achieve maximum participation and learning among all students. If there are significantly more boys than girls, boys tend to dominate the group.

Meece and McColskey also emphasize the need for groups to be closely monitored by teachers to ensure that they are functioning productively. They caution that "teachers should not assume that students know how to work together and cooperate." The problem of unequal contributions by students can be addressed by taking into account each member's performance and participation and basing evaluation "on some measure of improved performance so that everyone has an equal chance to contribute to the overall evaluation of the group" (Meece and McColskey).

Responsibility and Choice

Students need—and in most cases want—responsibility. In many instances, when students arrive at school nearly everything has already been decided for them. By and large, they are left out of the policy formation loop and they often have little say when it comes to the day-to-day functioning of both the classroom and the school. Rules are already in place and consequences preordained.

Although it may seem expedient to leave choice in the hands of teachers and administrators, failing to give students responsibility and choice dulls their motivation and reduces their level of commitment to one another and to the entire school community. Robbing students of responsibility and choice lessens their investment in learning. When students are not given a voice in the life of the school they are denied a plethora of opportunities to develop and then hone many personal qualities that will benefit them both in the present and in the future.

Douglas Heath (1994) implores school personnel to keep the needs of the whole person at the forefront and to rethink the scope of human excellence:

> Schools must provide opportunities for students to assume more meaningful responsibility for their own growth, not only within but also outside their walls. From their first day in school, students must be expected and taught how to be responsible for the growth of their minds, characters, and selves. Schools must recognize and reward the human excellence that results from valuing students' maturing as whole persons.

If schools are truly trying to educate the whole person, then offering students ample opportunities to exercise responsibility and choice will be a priority.

Meaning, Relevance, and Teaching Methods

Perhaps even more than in the past, students today question what they are being asked to learn and evaluate whether it makes sense, has a purpose, is something they believe to be useful or beneficial. Many students conclude that the curriculum leaves much to be desired. To a large extent, it is perceived as unimportant and lacking in value and relevance. This situation creates problems—for students, teachers, and, ultimately, for society.

Ron Brandt (1995) identifies student disenchantment with "the entrenched traditions of schooling" as perhaps the biggest challenge that is faced by educators today. He states,

> Some [students] see no connection whatever between their priorities and what teachers expect of them, so they disrupt lessons and refuse even to try. Others realize they must play the game, but go through the motions with minimal attachment to what they are supposedly learning. Teachers, thwarted by resistance or passivity, complain that students are unmotivated, and either search valiantly for novel approaches or resign themselves to routines they no longer expect to be productive.

Brandt asserts that "people learn when they have a reason," and he points out that although teaching certain content may make perfect sense in the eyes of teachers, students may not share their perspective. A critical component of teaching, contends Brandt, is "helping students find their own good reasons to learn."

What teachers choose to present and *how* they try to stimulate learning can of course make a major difference in students' level of motivation and engagement. Both the content that is selected and the format used to convey the content have an impact on the attitudes students develop toward school and the learning goals they adopt. As Martin Maehr, Carol Midgley, and Timothy Urdan (1992) state,

> The types of tasks that students undertake in the classroom can, in large part, determine the types of goals they will pursue and consequently their level of investment in school. For example, students can be given tasks that are relevant to their lives and require creative thinking and problems solving, or they can receive a daily dose of drill-and-practice dittos. In the former case, students are likely to value the task, adopt task-focused goals such as mastering the material, and be intrinsically motivated to do the task. In the case of the latter, students may perceive that the purpose of the task is merely to keep them busy, place little value on the activities involved, and adopt ability-focused goals such as looking smarter than their peers, leading to the use of surface-level strategies like finishing their work quickly regardless of the quality.

As Brophy (1986) notes, "We cannot expect students to be motivated to learn if we present them with pointless or meaningless activities." When burdened with a barrage of busywork and forced to complete uninteresting, unchallenging worksheets, students will probably perceive learning as rote, irrelevant repetition. Apathy and resentment may result from being forced to devote time to academic activities that are neither stimulating nor challenging. Boredom and resentment in turn often breed disruptive behavior. When severe, disenchantment with school may prompt students to prematurely end their formal education.

Lewis and colleagues argue that appropriate, relevant curriculum can be instrumental in reducing the need to offer extrinsic "payoffs" or incentives to students for engaging in academic work. "To minimize extrinsic rewards, educators need a curriculum that is worth learning and a pedagogy that helps students see why it is worth learning," they assert.

Unfortunately, in many instances the content with which students are presented is largely lacking in challenge and substance:

> Numerous critiques of the curriculum in this country argue that it sells children short by presenting material that is too simple and too easily mastered—for example, basal readers whose barren language and shallow ideas offer little reason to read. That a more challenging curriculum is more compelling to children, even so-called slow learners, is a tenet underlying some recent interventions (Hopfenberg 1993). (in Lewis and others)

Strong and colleagues asked both teachers and students two questions: What kind of work do you find totally engaging? and What kind of work do you hate to do? Respondents said engaging work "was work that stimulated their curiosity, permitted them to express their creativity, and fostered positive relationships with others. It was also work at which they were good." Conversely, respondents indicated they hated "work that was repetitive, that required little or no thought, and that was forced on them by others."

The following four goals play a major role in energizing engaged students, according to Strong and colleagues:

- Success (the need for mastery)
- Curiosity (the need for understanding)
- Originality (the need for self-expression)
- Relationships (the need for involvement with others)

These elements form the first four letters of SCORE, the acronym Strong and colleagues have given to their model of student engagement. Teachers should strive to cultivate all four goals when making instructional decisions. In combination, these four elements strengthen student engagement and produce Energy, the final letter in the acronym.

Strong and colleagues advise teachers to ask themselves the following questions when attempting to determine what students want and what motivates them:

1. Under what conditions are students most likely to feel that they can be successful?
2. When are students most likely to become curious?
3. How can we help students satisfy their natural drive toward self-expression?
4. How can we motivate students to learn by using their natural desire to create and foster good peer relationships?

If the curriculum features two defining characteristics, state Strong and others, it will be more apt to stimulate students' curiosity: (1) the information about a topic is fragmentary or contradictory, and (2) the topic relates to students' personal lives. When a body of information is disorganized, the very lack of organization creates a desire to make sense of it and put the disparate pieces together.

Strong and colleagues recommend that teachers ask themselves (or perhaps—even better—ask the students themselves): With what issues are adolescents wrestling? and How can we connect them to our curriculum? One example identified as an area of interest to adolescents is independence, the process of separating from parents and other adults. Strong and colleagues suggest that teachers make connections between students' personal quest for independence and autonomy and themes evident in material that is being studied. For example, when studying the American Revolution, a class might explore when rebellion is justified. Doing so would help establish a link between adolescents' personal concerns and issues that they may initially consider far removed from their own experience.

As mentioned earlier, both what is taught and how it is taught are important. Each affects how involved in the learning process students will be. Wlodkowski and Jaynes offer several suggestions related to both issues of content and process that have the potential to make learning more stimulating for students:

- Provide variety in learning.
- Relate learning to student interests.
- Use unpredictability within safe bounds for learning.
- Use novel and unusual teaching methods and content with students.
- Give students questions and tasks that get them thinking beyond rote memory.
- Have students actively participate in learning.
- Provide consistent feedback.
- Create learning experiences that have natural consequences or finished products.
- Use cooperative-learning techniques.
- Encourage student choice in the learning situation.
- Offer learning that is challenging.

In some cases, teachers can increase the relevance of content by presenting it in a timely manner. For example, if a teacher planned to cover the Middle East in May but military action involving the U.S. in that area of the world broke out in March, it might make sense for the teacher to adjust her original course plan. Reworking the teaching timeline would allow her to teach about the area during a period when student interest in the Middle East would probably be particularly strong (Raffini).

Raffini also asserts that it can be stimulating for students when teachers take an unpopular position on a subject, serving as a "devil's advocate." Having their beliefs and assumptions challenged can pull students into a discussion and cause them to think about why they have adopted a particular position on an issue. In addition, debating issues that have no "right" or "wrong" answers can facilitate active participation by students who might otherwise opt out of discussions for fear of offering a "wrong" answer.

If teachers are aware of students' hobbies, interests, and extracurricular activities, they can more readily relate instructional content to students' lives. Teachers can learn more about students' interests by having them fill out a questionnaire at the beginning of the year (Raffini). Although all content cannot be relevant to all students, if at least some of what is being taught is experienced as applicable to students' everyday lives or future goals, engagement will likely be higher.

While it is important for teachers to clearly organize their curricular goals and have projected timelines for covering particular content, they should avoid rigidity. For example, if students seem genuinely interested in a subject only indirectly related to the topic at hand, it can be useful for teachers to occasionally follow some of these spontaneously arising tangents and sacrifice continuity "to capitalize on student interest" (Raffini).

Task Difficulty

Students will be more or less motivated depending on the difficulty of the tasks that are presented to them. When making curricular decisions, teachers should strike an appropriate balance. Tasks should be neither so easy that they fail to present a challenge nor so difficult that they are unattainable. Teachers must avoid putting students in situations where they repeatedly try to master a task but are unable to do so. On the other hand, if a task is too easy, students will not derive feelings of increasing competence that a moderately challenging task provides.

There is no doubt that individualizing learning tasks to meet the needs of a classroom full of students with different skill levels is a significant challenge for the best of teachers. This challenge may be less daunting, however, in schools that group together students of different ages. Mixed-age classrooms can more readily address the needs of students whose performance tends to fall above or below the norm without making them feel separate from the rest of the class. An older student with weak reading skills, for example, could be grouped with younger classmates for subjects that rely heavily on reading skills and then be grouped with peers for subjects that are less dependent on reading skills, such as art.

In classrooms that are age-graded, teachers must be more innovative. In some instances, parents can be recruited to assist in the classroom. Peer tutors can also be an effective resource. Many programs have found that peer tutoring tends to result in academic gains for both tutors and tutees. A stronger sense of self-worth, confidence, and competence is often a byproduct of the experience for both members of such dyads.

Another method of dealing with individual differences is practiced in China. When designing and constructing assignments and tests, teachers include some problems that every member of the class will be able to solve and some problems that no one in the class will be able to solve, in addition to incorporating a number of moderately difficult problems that most students can solve (Stipek). This approach allows all students to experience some measure of success but at the same time beckons students to continue to strive for greater understanding and mastery.

Variety

We would quickly tire of eating the same thing for dinner night after night; if what was set before us never varied, we would soon stop looking forward to eating. Similarly, teachers cannot expect students to be eager to learn if what is offered to them is rote, repetitive, and lacking in variety. Students will not eagerly anticipate learning if they are expected to consume a bland, unchanging academic diet. Teachers can spice up students' academic diet by varying the teaching methods they use and giving students different types of assignments. Wlodkowski and Jaynes note that "well-timed changes in methods of instruction help students to pay attention and renew interest," while the absence of variation can cause students to feel that school is a "daily grind."

Although there is a place for the lecture format, teachers should not rely too heavily on this approach. If day after day students are expected to sit quietly and listen to teachers speak, this will shape their view of learning. Such an environment invites students to conclude that school is a place where they are expected to be passive vessels that merely take in and later regurgitate what comes out of teachers' mouths.

Small-group discussions, hands-on experiences, and student presentations and portfolios are examples of formats that require active student involvement. Active and interactive formats encourage students to interpret and make meaning out of what is being taught and then relate and integrate it to what they already know about the world. The learning that occurs under such circumstances will be rooted more deeply and retained more readily than when students are asked to complete reams of rote, repetitive worksheets.

Sometimes minor instructional changes can create major changes in student engagement. For example, in one classroom, after completing stories contained in a textbook, students were required to answer questions from the textbook. Most students showed little enthusiasm for this almost daily ritual. However, when the teacher altered the task one day by having the students generate their own questions and then exchange them with a classmate, student interest rose.

However, Phyllis Blumenfeld (1992) points out that teachers must use care when selecting activities to enliven the curriculum. If poorly conceived, attempts to breathe life into learning through variety may actually distract students from the content goals associated with the task. When actions taken to create variety are not closely linked with the primary thrust of the task, students may be enamored by one peripheral aspect of the task, but their cognitive engagement with the activity may actually decline.

Instructive Feedback

In some classrooms, the only feedback students get is letter grades, percentages, or points. Input about what they could do differently in the future or how to improve their performance is often the exception rather than the rule. While the data they are provided may give them a sense of their absolute performance in terms of how well they met the teacher's standards or expectations, the value of this type of information is limited in terms of its ability to guide improvement or inform future attempts. As Meece and McColskey note, students could benefit from more substantive feedback, particularly oral feedback that enables dialogue and exchange between teachers and students:

> Research and observation suggest that classrooms could get by with much less grading, judging, measuring of student performance and more commentary and descriptive feedback that tells the student that he or she is off track, without labeling the effort publicly. Oral feedback may be particularly underused in most classrooms. When it is used fully, the teacher appears to be coaching students, constantly encouraging them to try to articulate what they know, providing feedback on misconceptions, and reminding them of expectations.

By talking with students about their work and the processes they employ to arrive at answers or achieve certain goals, teachers can learn valuable information about students, including perhaps getting a glimpse of what sparks their interest and sets their motivational wheels in motion.

Student Self-Evaluation

Evaluation should not be limited to feedback and assessment from outside sources. If one of the goals of education is to make students responsible for their own learning, they must have repeated practice over time in accurately judging the quality of their own work. By encouraging the development of self-evaluation skills in their students, teachers move students closer to the center of the learning process and strengthen students' ability to assess their own work.

While the practices of some teachers seem to reflect a belief that, to be valid, evaluation must come from an outside source—most often themselves—other teachers make a concerted effort to promote the development of student responsibility for learning by building self-evaluation into the learning process. Marshall mentions one approach to strengthening students' ability to thoughtfully review their work.

In the classroom described by Marshall, students are required to attach cover sheets to their completed projects. These forms are used by the students to rate their projects on various dimensions. This process helps students to step back and look at their work with a more objective set of eyes. Once projects have been reviewed by their teacher, students are also able to compare how similar their own perceptions of the quality of their work are to the perceptions of their teacher. While one evaluator is not "wrong" and the other "right," recognition of points at which perspectives diverge can serve as grist for an exploration of which evaluative criteria were used by each party and why, and a discussion of the relative weight each person assigned to various elements that were evaluated.

Over time, students who engage in thoughtful self-evaluation will become increasingly skilled at recognizing what factors to attend to when creating and revising their own work. They will also become more adept at accurately appraising and constructively commenting on the work of others. In addition, students who are invited to engage in self-evaluation will be more likely to feel that they have a voice in the learning process and appreciate that their perspectives are both solicited and carefully considered. Self-evaluation will not only develop in students the ability to carefully analyze the strengths and weaknesses of their work but will also give them the message that what they think counts.

Attention to Both Mind and Character

If students are ultimately expected to function in society in a way that is both satisfying and responsible, the education of students must reach beyond the intellectual realm. Social/emotional and moral learning must be attended to as well. Although students' families are central in the development of character, schools, too, play an important role. Teachers and administrators must ask themselves if their mission is to turn out good students or good students who are also good people. Do we want them to succeed only in the classroom or to become satisfied, contributing, well-adjusted human beings?

If the goal is to foster individuals who have good character as well as good grades, then teachers as well as parents and community members must take a holistic approach to supporting students' development. As Lewis and colleagues remind us, "Everything about schooling—curriculum, teaching method, discipline, interpersonal relationships—teaches children about the human qualities that we value."

Heath recommends thinking about the concept of excellence broadly, rather than applying it only to academic pursuits, for students need more than good grades to become fulfilled, contributing members of society. As he states,

> Clearly, if we value human excellence as a goal for living—or for schooling—then we cannot ignore ethical values such as honesty, integrity, commitment, and fairness—not self-attributes such as openness, confidence, or reliability, nor cognitive strengths of intelligence, good judgment, and knowledgeability.

Heath contends that "single-minded emphasis on academic excellence obscures to students the centrality of their character to their future success." Even though teachers value character and self-development, for the most part, they

> shrink from assuming responsibility for their development. They already feel overloaded by their schools' academic demands. More pointedly, few have any ideas about how they might teach for character maturation

other than to use their lecterns as pulpits from which to sermonize and exhort. (Heath)

Focusing on issues related to what kinds of people students are in the process of becoming, and what kinds of people they want to be, as well as on traditional academic areas, will stimulate student motivation and benefit both society and the individuals passing through the school system. Such issues as how best to form and maintain relationships with others and how to bring moral/ethical reasoning to bear on a situation have a high degree of interest to students, particularly during adolescence, as self-awareness and identity issues come to the forefront.

To be maximally effective, education must engage and acknowledge the needs of the whole person. As Heath notes,

> Failure to provide students with the opportunity to learn simultaneously with their heads, hearts, and hands detaches knowledge from passion and power; students become one-dimensional, impotent to feel and act wholeheartedly.

Positive Peer Relations

The academic and social worlds of students are intertwined. Friends play a significant role in many areas of students' lives, and the influence of peers intensifies as students pass through adolescence. Students' choice of friends can affect their attitudes, values, and actions, and thus it is important to recognize that peer influence does not stop at the school door. Steinberg states,

> Our research indicates that peers shape student achievement patterns in profound ways, and that in many respects friends are more powerful influences than family members are. For a large number of adolescents, peers—not parents—are the chief determinants of how intensely they are invested in school and how much effort they devote to their education.

The influence of peers on student engagement and school performance does not suddenly materialize out of thin air during adolescence. Even in early elementary school, the quality of a students' peer relations is predictive of their academic performance.

Students who have difficulty getting along with their peers in the early years of school "have more long-term learning difficulties and academic problems" (Parke and others 1998). Many studies suggest that "low acceptance by peers through the early school years is associated with lower academic achievement in the late elementary and middle-school period" (Parke and others).

In a longitudinal study that spanned more than eight years, Parke and colleagues collected data from nine elementary schools. The study included more than 2,000 kindergarten children and their families and friends. Classroom social behavior and academic records were examined, and other measures of social and emotional characteristics were used to assess the students. Parke and colleagues looked at patterns and changes in the participants' social and academic behavior over time. Some of their findings are noted below:

- A link between social skills and academic performance was established.
- Lower levels of social acceptance in kindergarten were predictive of (1) deficits in classroom social skills and work habits in the first and second grades, and (2) lower academic performance as assessed by grades and standardized-achievement test scores in the first and second grades.
- "Social skills (getting along with peers) and academic competence influence each other consistently over time." A bidirectional pattern of influence between academic competence and social competence emerged.
- Rejection by peers was associated with academic problems in early elementary school. "Children who are stably rejected during the first two years of elementary school appear to be at risk for early academic difficulties relative to stably accepted children."
- Good relations with peers seems to set the stage for enhanced classroom behaviors, work habits, and academic achievement. "Stable acceptance by peers

over the early school years protects children from early academic difficulties. Acceptance appears to be associated with a constellation of positive social skills that serve" to protect children from later social difficulties with peers.

- "Children who are not actively rejected, but who are experiencing other forms of social difficulties, may also be at some risk for early academic difficulties." Some children display behaviors "similar to both socially popular and socially rejected children. They are perceived by their peers as disruptive and often as starting fights, but they are also leaders in the peer group." These children, who the researchers categorized as "controversial," are both strongly disliked and strongly liked by their classmates. "Children categorized as 'controversial' in kindergarten showed some degree of difficulty in first- and second-grade classroom behaviors, and the controversial boys performed more poorly than popular boys in second-grade mathematics."

- "Peer rejection in the early school years may be more systematically related to problematic classroom behaviors than to actual academic performance outcomes. Children with social difficulties may be at risk for later school failure because of less than optimal learning styles, such as spending less time on task, doing homework less often, and displaying poor planning and organizational skills." (Parke and others)

Parke and colleagues recommend that teachers try to be attuned to young students who are having difficulty socially with peers, because this may foreshadow future academic problems. If schools identify such students early on, they are in a better position to then offer intervention programs intended to enhance both their social and academic skills. By working to create positive relations among students and intervening in situations where students are not readily accepted by their peers, teachers and other school personnel can increase students' enjoyment of and commitment to schooling.

Peers' influence over one another can be either positive or negative in regard to school performance. Particularly during adolescence, when the power peers exert over one another is the most potent, the value one's friends place on academic effort and performance can indeed make a difference. As Steinberg notes, "At a time in development when children are especially susceptible to the power of peer influence, the circle of friends an adolescent can choose from may make all the difference between excellent and mediocre school performance."

As part of his longitudinal study of factors affecting student engagement, Steinberg tracked students throughout high school. His intent was to discover whether the performance of students who began high school with equivalent academic and behavioral profiles would be affected either positively or negatively by their selection of friends during high school. He found the answer to be a resounding yes.

Choice of peers influenced two areas in particular: academic performance and delinquency. On the positive side, among students who began high school with equivalent academic and behavioral profiles, those whose friends had higher grades, spent more time on homework, had higher educational aspirations, and were more involved in extracurricular activities "did better over the course of high school than students who had less academically-oriented friends" (Steinberg).

The more teachers can do to encourage positive relations among students and to model acceptance and respect for all students, the easier it will be for students to maintain their motivation to learn.

Look to Students for Input

Last, but not least, it is important for teachers to perceive of students as important sources of information about motivation. In some respects, students are the real experts. Though not often consulted about educational issues and problems, students have a perspective that cannot be gained from other sources. As Strong and colleagues note, "Imagine what could happen if we engaged our students in a discussion of... motivation. What might they tell us about themselves and their classrooms? Could we actually teach them to design their own work in ways that match their own unique potential for engagement?"

Sharon Newbill and Jeanne Stubbs (1997) also believe it is imperative for educators to ask questions such as, "What is the meaning of schooling for... students? How do students describe some of their experiences at school? and What influences shape these schooling experiences of students?" And the best way to get reliable answers is by asking students themselves.

Conclusion

Ultimately, motivation to learn resides within students themselves. However, teachers are in a prime position to support it through the attitudes they model (both about learning and toward students), the teaching methods they employ, and the curriculum they present.

5

SCHOOLWIDE STRATEGIES

Student motivation is affected greatly by what happens at a classroom level. Teachers can do much to cultivate a love of learning in their students and facilitate student engagement. However good practice at the classroom level can either be supported or thwarted by school- or district-level policies and practices. "The classroom is not an island" but rather part of a larger social system (Maehr and Midgley). Eric Anderman and Timothy Urdan (1995) stress that it is essential to recognize that "those in designated administrative positions play powerful roles in shaping a school's motivational culture."

School leaders and other administrators, as well as classroom teachers, have a responsibility to ensure that the educational environment students are exposed to is one that fosters motivation to learn. As Maehr, Midgley, and Urdan state, "Just as the smaller unit of the classroom has been found to define learning, it now appears that the larger unit of the school may likewise define learning and therewith have a pervasive influence on student motivation."

If school leaders and classroom teachers are both on the same page, so to speak, in terms of their views on learning and motivation, what's done at the school level will complement what's taking place in the classroom and vice versa. When classroom-, school-, and district-level policies and practices in regard to student motivation are aligned and mutually supportive, students will receive consistent rather than conflicting messages about the value and purposes of learning, and the impact of positive efforts at each level will be maximized.

Schoolwide Learning Goals

Much like individual classrooms, schools vary in the types of learning goals they emphasize. As Maehr and Midgley note, "Decisions, practices, and actions that have schoolwide effects are likely to symbolize the purposes and meaning of time spent in a particular school." For example, some schools "stress learning more for its own sake," while "others put special emphasis on extrinsic rewards and competition" (Maehr and Midgley).

Some school leaders intentionally downplay differences in the relative ability of students and minimize cross-student comparisons. Instead they communicate to students through their words and actions that effort is valued and that the purpose of learning is "to gain understanding, insight, or skill," not to outperform others. When leaders strive to communicate the latter message, they in turn are likely to influence the learning goals that students adopt, and thereby play "a profoundly important role in the determination of the nature and quality of student motivation and learning" (Maehr, Midgley, and Urdan).

Teachers as well as students are affected by the signals sent out at the school level. School-level policies and practices tend to encourage or restrict teachers' freedom to implement motivational strategies at a classroom level. In addition, school leaders are influential in creating the psychological climate of the school, which can either support or tear down teacher motivation and morale. In turn, teacher motivation and commitment affect student motivation, and vice versa.

Encouraging Curricular Creativity by Teachers

One area in which school leaders have input is in the nature of the academic tasks that are offered to students. Maehr, Midgley, and Urdan note that many effective principals directly involve themselves in decisions related to curriculum and instruction. Their hands-on style enables them to

> stress strict adherence to textbooks or encourage teachers to think broadly and creatively about academic

tasks including: interviewing knowledgeable persons, surveying constituencies, providing hands-on and project-oriented activities, allowing for independent study, facilitating field trips, and countless other possibilities.

Depending to some extent on the perspective of the principal, teachers can either feel tied to textbooks, worksheets, and preplanned exercises or feel free "to design and use tasks that are action-oriented, that flow from the interests of the students, and that are challenging and creative" (Maehr, Midgley, and Urdan). One of the primary ways school leaders can positively affect the environment of the school "is by encouraging teachers to take risks and be creative in designing instructional tasks" (Maehr, Midgley, and Urdan).

Providing Opportunities for Student Decision-Making

Another area identified by Maehr, Midgley, and Urdan as falling within the scope of school leaders' influence is promoting student initiative and responsibility. Schools differ in the degree of choice students have over what they learn and how they learn. Through their involvement in setting schoolwide rules and guidelines, principals play a major role in determining how much of a "voice" students have in the daily life of the school. Principals can "focus on controlling behavior by putting limitations on students and developing rules to control students, or they can develop ways to give students more choice, initiative, and responsibility" (Maehr, Midgley, and Urdan). The authors note that either emphasis is likely to have implications for the conclusions students draw about "the nature of the school's mission, its relevance to their lives, and the intrinsic work of learning."

Defining What Is Worthy of Recognition and Reward

Under what circumstances praise and accolades are given to students is also controlled to some degree by school leaders. For example, if an honor roll is the only way a school acknowledges student achievement, the message students may come away with is that high grades are valued, not improvement, progress, or discovery. And while all students are capable of improvement, all students are not equally capable of achieving grades that will earn them a spot on the honor roll. If attaining a place on the honor roll is their only chance to "shine," some students will never receive recognition for their engagement in the learning process.

Debra Viadero (1999) contends, "In schools and classrooms that rank or compare students in very public ways, children avoid asking teachers for help or brag that they put off studying for tests until the last minute."

School leaders may benefit from examining how they can broaden, or perhaps even completely rethink, what they acknowledge and why. It is important to consider how to honor improvement, effort, progress, and academic "personal bests" as well as recognizing those who consistently attain high grades and exhibit exemplary academic performance.

In addition to exercising care in what is acknowledged, care must also be taken in how rewards and privileges are devised and doled out. Maehr, Midgley, and Urdan illustrate by noting one school in which the "reward" students received for good conduct was being allowed to skip fifteen minutes of "their most dreaded class." This "reward" obviously contradicts the idea of learning as valuable.

Another "well-meaning" school-based program sponsored by a pizza chain rewards students with pizza based on how many books they read. In this case, state Maehr and colleagues, "students compete with each other, recognition is on the basis of relative ability, and the difficulty or challenge inherent in the task is ignored." Teachers reported to Maehr and others that most students "read the easiest, shortest books they can find." (As Lewis and others note, "One sage commentator quipped, 'If we want children to read books, we should offer them books as a reward for eating pizzas, not pizzas for reading books.' ") The bottom line is that administrators must be aware they "can and do affect how learning is perceived in the school through the recognition practices they promote or accede to" (Maehr, Midgley, and Urdan).

Examining Grouping Practices and Resource Allocation

Grouping students by ability can have many detrimental effects, as mentioned earlier. For example, teachers may adjust their expectations downward with lower ability students, rather than maintaining high expectations and altering other variables, such as time needed for mastery to occur. Students' self-perceptions are also affected by their placement in homogeneous groups. As Maehr and colleagues note, "Students assigned to low ability groups or classes are well aware that they are considered inferior to students in higher ability groups."

In many cases, inequitable resource allocation also accompanies the practice of ability grouping. For example, access to computers may be reserved for higher ability groups or the ways in which computers are used may differ dramatically. In higher level groups and classes, students may "use the computer for desk top publishing, for simulations, for programming, and for complex problem solving," while in lower level groups students "typically use drill and practice software that gives them immediate feedback but fails to either motivate them or to develop higher order thinking skills" (Maehr, Midgley, and Urdan).

Maehr and colleagues note that school leaders "exert considerable influence over policies that encourage or discourage homogeneous grouping." They recommend that principals stimulate "thoughtful discussion about the pros and cons of ability grouping" by organizing appropriate inservice training and providing teachers with summaries of relevant research findings regarding grouping practices. At a minimum, they encourage school leaders to review "precisely how resources are assigned to different groups" and determine if adjustments need to be made. As they note, "Teachers and students are sensitive to how resources are allocated, particularly since most schools operate on limited budgets, and in this way come to understand what is valued and not valued in the school."

Assessing Evaluation Practices

School leaders as well as classroom teachers influence how students are evaluated and how evaluation data are interpreted. Classroom-level evaluation decisions are "heavily influenced by school leaders," according to Maehr, Midgley, and Urdan. More often than not, evaluation practices tend to define learning as competitive contests "in which some win and others lose" (Maehr, Midgley, and Urdan).

Through how they treat evaluation at the school level, principals can set a standard for teachers to follow. Principals can be pivotal in emphasizing student effort and progress and in viewing the results of evaluation as a springboard for setting new learning goals, not as a means of separating the "best" and the "brightest" from the rest (Maehr, Midgley, and Urdan).

In many school districts, the administration of tests and the assignment of letter grades may be non-negotiable elements. Even so, principals have "significant control" over how such data are interpreted and framed (Maehr, Midgley, and Urdan). Subtly or not so subtly, principals attach various shades of meaning to these practices, thereby affecting "how students perceive learning and schooling and how they feel about themselves" (Maehr, Midgley, and Urdan).

Some specific steps school leaders can take to influence the meaning that is attached to evaluation by both teachers and students include exposing teachers to alternative forms of evaluation through inservice training, establishing guidelines for how evaluative data are reported to parents, and providing school-level recognition of progress and improvement as well as high achievement.

Making Scheduling Decisions

How the school day is divided has far-reaching implications. Scheduling influences how students are grouped, whether team teaching and interdisciplinary approaches to curriculum are feasible, whether hands-on, project-based methods of instruction are viable options, and whether field trips and other opportunities to learn outside the school walls are possible (Maehr, Midgley, and Urdan).

If the school day is inflexible and cut into a series of forty-five- or fifty-minute segments, many potentially more engaging approaches to teaching and learning are difficult if not impossible to pursue. Fifty-minute periods are conducive to a lecture format and a "didactic, teacher-oriented approach to instruction" (Maehr, Midgley, and Urdan). Conversely, when the school schedule is more adaptable or flexible, it "permits a broader range of freedom and self-determination for both teachers and students" and "facilitates more engaging approaches to the curriculum, including interdisciplinary, project-oriented activities, and learning tasks in which the student can assume some ownership and derive personal meaning" (Maehr, Midgley, and Urdan). In turn, the types of teaching strategies made possible by more flexible scheduling allow greater emphasis on "task" rather than "ability" goals.

As Maehr, Midgley, and Urdan emphasize, division of the school day is an administrative matter that typically falls within the domain of school leaders. They suggest that principals seek to adapt the school schedule to best meet teacher and student needs. By making scheduling decisions that facilitate more engaging forms of teaching, school leaders have the ability to positively affect student motivation (Maehr, Midgley, and Urdan).

Creating Smaller Centers of Learning

Considerable research points to the positive effects of small schools on students' attitudes toward learning (Educational Research Service 1998). In smaller settings, students perceive of schools as more caring, and they tend to feel less alienated. Conversely, as Heath notes, "Once an elementary school has more than about 200 to 350 students and an upper school 400 to 500 or more, a host of potentially unhealthy effects become noticeable, especially for vulnerable kids."

Officials at East Forsyth High School in Winston-Salem, North Carolina, noted that ninth-graders had four times as many discipline problems as their older high school classmates and also had the highest percentage of dropouts and failures of the four high school grades. School leaders instituted several strategies to ease the transition of ninth-graders into high school. One change consisted of assigning every ninth-grader a teacher advocate "to look after them." Each teacher at the school had nine or ten students for whom they served as advocates (Meece and McColskey). This personalized the school for students as they made the transition into high school and gave the students consistent access to a specific staff member.

Another strategy designed to make the school seem smaller and less overwhelming was the decision to designate two buildings as freshman buildings. The goal was to enable ninth-graders to feel "less intimidated by older students when changing classes" (Meece and McColskey). This example illustrates a few of the ways school leaders can give their school a smaller, more personal "feel" even if the size of the school is not able to be reduced.

Even though school leaders may not be able to reduce the size of their schools, they can be instrumental in enhancing student motivation and engagement by subdividing the learning environment and providing avenues for more sustained student-teacher contact through the formation of schools-within-schools, minischools, and house plans. As Mary Anne Raywid (1996) notes, finding ways of downsizing schools can foster students' sense of belonging and enlarge their capacity to act as "engaged and committed agents in their own and others' education."

Maintaining a Motivational Climate for Teachers and Students

The nature and quality of interactions that occur between principals and teachers are related to the nature and quality of interactions that develop between teachers and students. If principals create an environment that helps teachers to remain motivated and enjoy high morale, it is more likely that students, in turn, will be more motivated and engaged. As Grossnickle and Thiel state, "Principals serve as gatekeepers and motivators of the motivators (teachers) in facilitating a motivating school environment."

Achieving Better Alignment Between School Environment and Student Needs

As students develop, their capacity to evaluate what people are expecting of them, both academically and behaviorally, increases. They become better able to assess and draw conclusions about whether what is being asked of them is worthwhile or relevant from their perspective. By the time they reach middle school, many students begin to question and reflect upon what they are being offered at school and make judgments about whether it is meaningful and makes sense.

Unfortunately, as students' analytical abilities increase, their motivation to learn at school often decreases. It is common for students to experience a drop in motivation in their initial year of middle school or junior high school. As Jacquelynne Eccles and others (1993) report, "Research suggests that the early adolescent years mark the beginning of a downward spiral for some individuals, a spiral that leads some adolescents to academic failure and school dropout." Eccles and colleagues cite evidence of a "marked decline in some early adolescents' school grades as they move into junior high school."

In addition, interest in school, intrinsic motivation, self-concept, and self-perception, and confidence in one's intellectual ability are all areas that are more likely to decline during adolescence (Eccles and others). Conversely, a cluster of other factors that impede learning—including test anxiety, learned helplessness responses to failure, truancy, and school dropout—are more prevalent among adolescents than among younger students (Eccles and others).

Eccles and colleagues suggest that schools may play a contributing role in the deterioration that occurs in many early adolescents' school-related motivation. They note that research "in a variety of areas has documented the impact of classroom and school environmental characteristics on motivation." According to Eccles and colleagues, "Some of the motivational problems seen at early adolescence may be a consequence of the negative changes in the school environment rather than characteristics of the developmental period per se."

Eccles and others contend that a poor "fit" or a "mismatch" exists between adolescents' developmental needs and several aspects of the school environment. Motivational problems emerge, they assert, when individuals "are in environments that do not fit well with their needs"

(Eccles and others). In many cases, during junior high or middle school "there are developmentally inappropriate changes in a cluster of classroom organizational, instructional, and climate variables, including task structure, task complexity, grouping practices, evaluation techniques, motivational strategies, locus of responsibility for learning, and quality of teacher-student and student-student relationships" (Eccles and others).

In particular, Eccles and colleagues identify six fundamental differences between elementary and junior high or middle schools that may contribute to motivational problems among early adolescents:

1. Compared with elementary school classrooms, junior high schools have a "greater emphasis on teacher control and discipline, and fewer opportunities for student decision-making, choice, and self-management." A greater proportion of junior high school teachers' school day is spent engaged in behavior management compared with that of elementary school teachers. The authors' own research indicates that opportunities for students to participate in decision-making also tend to be more restricted during junior high compared to the upper elementary grades.

2. There are also generally "less personal and less positive" relationships between teachers and students in junior high classrooms compared to elementary classrooms. In one study (Carol Midgley and others 1988), students and observers both rated junior high school math teachers "less friendly, less supportive, and less caring than the teachers these students had one year earlier in the last year of elementary school."

3. At the junior high level, there is also an increase in "practices such as whole-class task organization, between-classroom ability grouping, and public evaluation of the correctness of work." Whereas sixth-grade elementary school teachers are likely to use a mix of both whole-group and small-group instruction, among seventh-grade teachers small-group instruction is rare.

4. Junior high teachers "feel less effective" as teachers than do elementary school teachers, especially in

relation to low-ability students. In one study by Carol Midgley, Harriet Feldlaufer, and Jacquelynne Eccles (1989), seventh-grade mathematics teachers reported much lower confidence than did their sixth-grade elementary school counterparts in the same district, even though the seventh-grade teachers were more likely to be math specialists.

5. Classwork during the initial year of junior high tends to require lower, rather than higher, cognitive skills than does classwork provided during elementary school. In one study of science teachers cited by Eccles and others, the most frequent activity "involved copying answers from the board or textbook onto worksheets."

6. Junior high or middle school teachers also appear to use a higher standard in judging students' competence and in attaching letter grades to their work. One study cited by Eccles and others found 54 percent of students experienced a decline in grades during their first year of junior high. However, "the decline in grades is not. . . accompanied by a similar decline in the adolescents' scores on standardized achievement tests, which suggests that the decline reflects a change in grading practices rather than a change in the rate of the students' learning" (Eccles and others).

Eccles and colleagues note that the six tendencies cited above "are likely to have a negative effect on children's motivational orientation toward school at any grade level," but the magnitude of the ill effects are potentially greater for early adolescents because of their emerging developmental needs. As Eccles and others note,

> The environmental changes often associated with transition to junior high school seem especially harmful in that they emphasize competition, social comparison, and ability self-assessment at a time of heightened self-focus; they decrease decision making and choice at a time when the desire for control is growing; they emphasize lower level cognitive strategies at a time when the ability to use higher level strategies is in-

creasing; and they disrupt social networks at a time when adolescents are especially concerned with peer relationships and may be in special need of close adult relationships outside of the home. We believe the nature of these environmental changes, coupled with the normal course of individual development, results in a developmental mismatch so that the fit between the early adolescent and the classroom environment is particularly poor, increasing the risk of negative motivational outcomes, especially for adolescents who are having difficulty succeeding in school academically.

Conversely, when junior high schools and middle schools are more closely aligned with the developmental needs of early adolescents and offer positive and appropriate learning environments—that is, when classrooms and schools are characterized by higher teacher efficacy, more (and more substantial) opportunities for student involvement in classroom- and school-level decision-making, and positive student-teacher relationships—students "do not demonstrate the same declines in intrinsic motivation and school attachment stereotypically associated with students in junior high schools." In addition, schools in which there is a better "fit" between adolescents' developmental needs and the learning environment tend to experience fewer behavioral problems or instances of student misconduct.

Organization of Curriculum

Because the curriculum of American schools has traditionally tended to be organized in a specific way, there is a tendency not to consider other possible frameworks that may mesh better with students' developmental needs, particularly the needs of middle and high school students, where more serious motivational problems tend to surface.

According to Heath, the curriculum of most middle or junior high schools "is too fragmented and departmentally organized as well as too abstract and remote from students' interest and experience." He asserts that students need schools whose interpersonal climates are empathic, accepting, and caring and that offer a "more thematically organized curriculum attuned to their interests." Teachers can benefit from asking, What are the evolving natural interests of this age group?

Heath identifies central issues of early adolescents as "their changing bodies and sexuality, authority, law, power, friendships and group relationships, conflict-resolving and negotiating skills, environmental issues, and the world over the immediate horizon waiting to be explored." Students are motivated to find out who they are, to discover how to be in the world. These needs, being personally salient for students, can help to guide how curriculum is organized, particularly at the middle and high school levels, where serious motivational problems are most prevalent.

According to Heath, when students enter middle school or junior high school in sixth or seventh grade, "their morale, particularly boys', precipitously declines... and then stumbles along at about the same level from eighth through twelfth grade. The pubertal years begin to generate increasing numbers of future dropouts." He believes what is needed is "a more action- or experientially-based curriculum" that takes advantage of middle-school students' high energy level. Heath states that students "should not be sitting in chairs five periods a day being talked at, reading textbooks, or just doing problems. They should also be purposefully moving around, interacting and working with and teaching and learning from other students, and exploring their environmental, vocational and service world."

James Beane (1993) likewise suggests that a change in how middle-school curriculum is organized could make school more engaging for students. He recommends structuring the curricular content around the intersection of personal and social concerns that are relevant to early adolescents. Listed below are some of the issues and concerns Beane identifies as particularly important to adolescents. He believes these issues should inform curricular decisions:

1. Understanding and dealing with physical, intellectual, and socio-emotional changes, how they fit within lifespan development, and their implications for personal and social living

2. Developing a sense of personal identity, including a clear self-concept, positive self-esteem, and the ways in which self-perceptions are formed and how they influence attitudes and behaviors in social interactions

3. Exploring questions of values, morals, and ethics in immediate and distant social relationships, and with regard to the form and function of social institutions

4. Finding a place and securing some level of status in the peer group as well as understanding how the peer group forms and operates

5. Developing a personally acceptable balance between independence from adult authority figures and continuing dependence on them for various kinds of security

6. Dealing with the dizzying array of commercial interests that are aimed at early adolescents, including those related to fashion, music, leisure activities, and the like

7. Negotiating the maze of multiple expectations in the home, the school, the peer group, and other settings of everyday life

8. Developing commitments to people and causes in order to form a sense of self-worth, affirmation, achievement, and efficacy

Although Beane acknowledges most adolescents would probably not articulate their personal concerns in quite the way they are stated above, he argues that "if we watch and talk to them very carefully, instead of just talking *about* them, we are likely to see these concerns running through a great deal of what they say and do."

In addition to personal concerns, the other major organizing category of the two-pronged general-education curriculum Beane proposes for middle schools is social concerns. He reminds us that early adolescents are "real people living out real lives in a very real world." As such, they are aware of—and have often experienced firsthand—issues such as "poverty, homelessness, pollution, and racism." Examples of the types of social issues around which a general-education curriculum could be structured, according to Beane, include the following:

1. Interdependence among peoples in multiple layers from the immediate network of relationships to the global level
2. The diversity of cultures that are present within each of those layers, formed by race, ethnicity, gender, geographic region, and other factors
3. Problems in the environment that range from diminishing resources to disposal of waste and that come together in the question of whether we can sustain a livable planet
4. Political processes and structures, including their contradictions, that have simultaneously liberated and oppressed particular groups of people
5. Economic problems ranging from personal economic security to increasing commercialization of interests to the issue of inequitable distribution of wealth and related power
6. The place of technology as it enters into various aspects of life, and the moral issues it presents
7. The increasing incidence of self-destructive behaviors including substance abuse, crime, adolescent pregnancies, participation in street gangs, and attempted and actual suicides

Beane contends there is considerable overlap between early adolescents' personal concerns and the broader social concerns. As he notes, "concerns in one or the other category are frequently micro or macro versions of each other." Displayed in Table 2 is an example provided by Beane of how personal and social concerns intersect and produce themes around which a curriculum can be organized.

Conclusion

Student motivation may initially be thought of as an issue that concerns only students and teachers. As seen in

TABLE 2

Intersections of Personal and Social Concerns (Sample)

Early Adolescent Concerns	Curriculum Themes	Social Concerns
Understanding personal changes	TRANSITIONS	Living in a changing world
Developing a personal identity	IDENTITIES	Cultural diversity
Finding a place in the group	INTERDEPENDENCE	Global interdependence
Personal fitness	WELLNESS	Environmental protection
Social status (e.g., among peers)	SOCIAL STRUCTURES	Class systems (by age, economics, etc.)
Dealing with adults	INDEPENDENCE	Human rights
Peer conflict and gangs	CONFLICT RESOLUTION	Global conflict
Commercial pressures	COMMERCIALISM	Effects of media
Questioning authority	JUSTICE	Laws and social customs
Personal friendships	CARING	Social welfare
Living in the school	INSTITUTIONS	Social institutions

Reprinted by permission of the author from Beane, J. (1993) *A Middle School Curriculum: From Rhetoric to Reality* (2nd ed.). Columbus, OH: National Middle School Association.

this chapter, however, there is also much school leaders can contribute when it comes to making schools more motivational learning environments. If principals keep the issue of motivation before them when making school-level decisions and setting schoolwide policies and practices, they can make learning a more appealing venture for all students.

CONCLUSION

When I began immersing myself in the literature, it quickly became apparent that the boundaries of human motivation are difficult to draw, since a seemingly endless number of variables affect why people choose to—or elect not to—invest their energy in particular pursuits. Numerous conceptual tendrils seem to extend outward from motivation and entwine themselves around still other elements. Because motivation is a complex construct that is closely linked to other areas, knowing how far to proceed down a particular path without getting lost or off-track was often challenging. Despite its unwieldy nature, however, motivation is an issue that is too important to be ignored.

Ron Brandt identifies the fact that "students are not in tune with the entrenched traditions of schooling" as one of the biggest challenges facing educators today. He notes that many students "see no connection whatever between their priorities and what teachers expect of them, so they disrupt lessons and refuse even to try," while others superficially "play the game" but demonstrate "minimal attachment to what they are supposedly learning." In turn, "teachers complain that students are unmotivated, and either search valiantly for novel approaches or resign themselves to routines they no longer expect to be productive."

If in responding to this crisis in motivation, educators merely try to jazz up students' educational diets or force feed them all kinds of reasons for partaking in learning, educators' efforts will ultimately come to nought. The outcome will be comparable to trying to get an infant to eat pureed vegetables. Students will either refuse to open their mouths or spit back out what they are being urged to swallow, no matter how sweetly they are smiled at or how soothingly they are coaxed.

What will ultimately be most beneficial is for educators to help students "find their own good reasons to learn" (Brandt). When contemplating the issue of student motivation, teachers and administrators may do well to bear in mind the Latin derivation of *educate*. Literally meaning "to lead," "to bring out," "to draw out," the word is antithetical to the idea of external sources attempting to foist information, ideas, or interest upon students. The term implies that an educator's role should be to help elicit what already resides within students—in this case, a passion for learning.

Principals can stand in front of their student bodies, and teachers in front of their classes, with the confidence that resident in every student is a passion to learn. In some students, that passion has become dormant, but it is still there, waiting to be quickened, called forth by adults who will care, listen, challenge, believe. Today's educators face a great opportunity and responsibility: To make learning something students will want to incline their hearts toward for their own personal reasons.

BIBLIOGRAPHY

Many of the items in this bibliography are indexed in ERIC's monthly catalog *Resources in Education* (*RIE*). Reports in *RIE* are indicated by an "ED" number. Journal articles, indexed in ERIC's companion catalog, *Current Index to Journals in Education*, are indicated by an "EJ" number.

Most items with an ED number are available from ERIC Document Reproduction Service (EDRS), 7420 Fullerton Rd., Suite 110, Springfield, VA 22153-2852.

To order from EDRS, specify the ED number, type of reproduction desired—microfiche (MF) or paper copy (PC), and number of copies. Add postage to the cost of all orders and include check or money order payable to EDRS. For credit card orders, call 1-800-443-3742.

Ames, Carole A. "Classrooms: Goals, Structures, and Student Motivation." *Journal of Educational Psychology* 84, 3 (September 1992): 261-71. EJ 452 395.

_____. "Motivation: What Teachers Need To Know." *Teachers College Record* 91, 3 (Spring 1990): 409-21.

Ames, Carole, and Russell Ames. *Research on Motivation in Education. Volume 1. Student Motivation.* Orlando, Florida: Academic Press, 1984.

Ames, Carole, and Jennifer Archer. "Achievement Goals in the Classroom: Students' Learning Strategies and Motivation Processes." *Journal of Educational Psychology* 80, 3 (September 1988): 260-67. EJ 388 054.

Anderman, Eric, and Timothy Urdan. "A Multilevel Approach to Middle-Level Reform." *Principal* 74, 3 (January 1995): 26-28. EJ 496 199.

Beane, James A. *A Middle School Curriculum: From Rhetoric to Reality.* Second Edition. Columbus, Ohio: National Middle School Association, 1993. 116 pages.

Blumenfeld, Phyllis C. "Classroom Learning and Motivation: Clarifying and Expanding Goal Theory." *Journal of Educational Psychology* 84, 3 (September 1992): 272-81. EJ 452 396.

Bosworth, Kris. "Caring for Others and Being Cared For: Students Talk Caring in School." *Phi Delta Kappan* 76, 9 (May 1995): 686-93. EJ 502 935.

Brandt, Ron. "Overview: Why People Learn." *Educational Leadership* 53, 1 (September 1995): 7.

Brophy, Jere. "Classroom Management and Learning." *American Education* 18, 2 (March 1982): 20-23. EJ 262 773.

_____. *On Motivating Students*. Occasional Paper No. 101. East Lansing, Michigan: Institute for Research on Teaching, Michigan State University, October 1986. 73 pages. ED 276 724.

_____. "Synthesis of Research on Strategies for Motivating Students To Learn." *Educational Leadership* (October 1987): 40-48. EJ 362 226.

Chandler, Kathryn; Mary Jo Nolin; and Nicholas Zill. *Parent and Student Perceptions of the Learning Environment at School*. Statistics in Brief. Washington, D.C.: National Center for Education Statistics, September 1993. 17 pages. ED 361 882.

Chaskin, Robert J., and Diana Mendley Rauner. "Youth and Caring: An Introduction." *Phi Delta Kappan* 76, 9 (May 1995): 667-74. EJ 502 932.

Condry, J., and J. Chambers. "Intrinsic Motivation and the Process of Learning." In *The Hidden Costs of Reward*, edited by M. R. Lepper and D. Greene. 61-84. Hillsdale, New Jersey: Lawrence Erlbaum Associates, Inc., 1978.

Corno, Lyn. "Encouraging Students To Take Responsibility for Learning and Performance." *The Elementary School Journal* 93, 1 (September 1992): 69-83. EJ 453 441.

Covington, Martin. "The Motive for Self-Worth." In *Research on Motivation in Education. Volume 1. Student Motivation*, edited by Russell E. Ames and Carole Ames. Orlando, Florida: Academic Press, 1984. 340 pages.

de Charms, Richard. *Enhancing Motivation: Change in the Classroom*. New York: Irvington, 1976. 279 pages.

Developmental Studies Center. *Ways We Want Our Class To Be: Class Meetings That Build Commitment to Kindness and Learning*. Oakland, California: Author, 1995. 120 pages.

Dodd, Anne Wescott. "Engaging Students: What I Learned Along the Way." *Educational Leadership* 53, 1 (September 1995): 65-67. EJ 511 728.

Eccles, Jacquelynne S.; Carol Midgley; Allan Wigfield; Christy Miller Buchanan; David Reuman; Constance Flanagan; and Douglas MacIver. "Development During Adolescence: The Impact of Stage-Environment Fit on Young Adolescents' Experiences in Schools and in Families." *American Psychologist* 48, 2 (February 1993): 90-101.

Educational Research Service. "Enhancing Student Engagement in Learning." *The Informed Educator Series*. Arlington, Virginia: Author, 1998.

Firestone, William A.; Sheila Rosenblum; and Arnold Webb. *Student and Teacher Commitment: One Key to School Effectiveness*. Philadelphia, Pennsylvania: Research for Better Schools, 1990. 94 pages.

Gardner, Howard, and Joseph Walters. "A Rounded Version." 13-34. In *Multiple Intelligences: The Theory in Practice*, by Howard Gardner. New York: Basic Books, 1993. 304 pages.

Grossnickle, Donald R., and William B. Thiel. *Promoting Effective Student Motivation in School and Classroom: A Practitioner's Perspective*. Reston, Virginia: National Association of Secondary School Principals, 1988. 72 pages. ED 290 716.

Heath, Douglas H. *Schools of Hope: Developing Mind and Character in Today's Youth*. San Francisco: Jossey-Bass, 1994. 444 pages. ED 386 813.

Hopfenberg, Wendy, and others. *The Accelerated Schools Resource Guide*. San Francisco: Jossey-Bass, 1993. 369 pages.

Johnson, Jean, and Steve Farkas, with Ali Bers. *Getting By: What American Teenagers Really Think About Their Schools*. Public Agenda, 1997. 54 pages. ED 404 756.

Lepper, Mark R. "Motivational Considerations in the Study of Instruction." *Cognition and Instruction* 5, 4 (1988): 289-309.

Lewis, Catherine. *Educating Hearts and Minds: Reflections on Japanese Preschool and Elementary Education*. New York: Cambridge University Press, 1995.

_____. "The Journey of Change: Case Study of a Successful School Reform Site." Oakland, California: Developmental Studies Center, forthcoming.

Lewis, Catherine C.; Eric Schaps; and Marilyn S. Watson. "The Caring Classroom's Academic Edge." *Educational Leadership* 54, 1 (September 1996): 16-21. EJ 530 625.

Lipsitz, Joan. "Prologue: Why We Should Care About Caring." *Phi Delta Kappan* 76, 9 (May 1995): 665-66.

Lumsden, Linda. "Motivating Today's Students: The Same Old Stuff Just Doesn't Work." *Portraits of Success Series.* Eugene, Oregon: ERIC Clearinghouse on Educational Management, 1996. 8 pages.

Maehr, Martin L. "Meaning and Motivation: Toward a Theory of Personal Investment." In *Research on Motivation in Education. Volume 1. Student Motivation,* edited by Russell E. Ames and Carole Ames. Orlando, Florida: Academic Press, 1984. 340 pages. ED 355 637.

Maehr, Martin L., and Carol Midgley. "Enhancing Student Motivation: A Schoolwide Approach." *Educational Psychologist* 26, 3 and 4 (1991): 399-427.

Maehr, Martin L.; Carol Midgley; and Timothy Urdan. *School Leader As Motivator.* Occasional Papers: School Leadership and Education Reform. Urbana, Illinois: National Center for School Leadership. 27 pages. 1992. ED 355 637.

Marshall, Hermine H. "Motivational Strategies of Three Fifth-Grade Teachers." *The Elementary School Journal* 88, 2 (November 1987): 135-50. EJ 362 747.

Meece, Judith, and Wendy McColskey. *Improving Student Motivation: A Guide for Teachers and School Improvement Teams.* Tallahassee, Florida: Southeastern Regional Vision for Education (SERVE), 1997. 107 pages. ED 410 197.

Midgley, Carol; Harriet Feldlaufer; and Jacquelynne Eccles. "Change in Teacher Efficacy and Student Self- and Task-Related Beliefs in Mathematics During the Transition to Junior High School." *Journal of Educational Psychology* 81, 2 (June 1989): 247-58. EJ 398 506.

Midgley, Carol, and others. *Student/Teacher Relations and Attitudes Toward Mathematics Before and After the Transition to Junior High School,* 1988. 25 pages. ED 301 477.

Motsinger, Hillery. "Recipe for Success: Factors That Help Students To Succeed." *NASSP Bulletin* 77, 554 (September 1993): 6-15. EJ 468 668.

Newbill, Sharon, and Jeanne Stubbs. "Interactive Spheres of Influence: A High School Culture." Paper presented at the Annual Meeting of the American Educational Research Association, Chicago, Illinois, March 24-28, 1997. 20 pages. ED 412 613.

Nicholls, John. "Conceptions of Ability and Achievement Motivation." In *Research on Motivation in Education. Volume 1. Student Motivation*, edited by Russell E. Ames and Carole Ames. Orlando, Florida: Academic Press, 1984. 340 pages.

Noblit, George; Dwight Rogers; and Brian McCadden. "In the Meantime: The Possibilities of Caring." *Phi Delta Kappan* 76, 9 (May 1995): 680-85. EJ 502 934.

Noddings, Nel. "Teaching Themes of Care." *Phi Delta Kappan* 76, 9 (May 1995): 675-79. EJ 502 933.

Nolen, Susan Bobbitt. "Reasons for Studying: Motivational Orientations and Study Strategies." *Cognition and Instruction* 5, 4 (1988).

Palmer, Parker. *To Know as We Are Known: A Spirituality of Education.* San Francisco: Harper and Row, 1983. 130 pages.

Parke Ross D.; Karen Harshman; Benita Roberts; Mary Flyr; Robin O'Neil; Mara Welsh; and Christine Strand. "Social Relationships and Academic Success." *Thrust for Educational Leadership* (September 1998): 32-34.

Poplin, Mary, and Joseph Weeres. *Voices from the Inside: A Report on Schooling from Inside the Classroom.* Claremont, California: Institute for Education in Transformation, Claremont Graduate School, 1992. 68 pages.

Raffini, James P. *Winners Without Losers: Structures and Strategies for Increasing Student Motivation To Learn.* Boston: Allyn and Bacon, 1993. 286 pages. ED 362 952.

Ravitch, Diane. *National Standards in American Education: A Citizen's Guide.* Washington, D.C.: Brookings Institution, 1995. 223 pages. ED 400 617.

Raywid, Mary Anne. *Taking Stock: The Movement to Create Mini-Schools, Schools-Within-Schools, and Separate Small Schools.* New York: ERIC Clearinghouse on Urban Education, April 1996. 72 pages. ED 396 045.

Solomon, D.; V. Battistich; M. Watson; E. Schaps; and C. Lewis. "A Six-District Study of Educational Change: Direct and Mediated Effects of the Child Development Project." Oakland, California: Developmental Studies Center, forthcoming.

Steinberg, Laurence. *Beyond the Classroom: Why School Reform Has Failed and What Parents Need To Do.* New York: Simon and Schuster, 1996. 223 pages. ED 398 346.

Stipek, Deborah. "The Development of Achievement Motivation." In *Research on Motivation in Education. Volume 1. Student Motivation,* edited by Russell E. Ames and Carole Ames. Orlando, Florida: Academic Press, 1984. 340 pages.

Strong, Richard; Harvey F. Silver; and Amy Robinson. "What Do Students Want (and What Really Motivates Them)?" *Educational Leadership* 53, 1 (September 1995): 8-12. EJ 511 713.

Viadero, Debra. "Lighting the Flame." *Education Week* XVIII, 22 (February 10, 1999): 24-26.

Vito, R.C.; W. Crichlow; and L. Johnson. "Motivational Characteristics of Academically Disaffected and Engaged Urban Junior High and High School Students." Paper presented at the Annual Meeting of the American Educational Research Association, San Francisco, March 1989.

Wasley, Patricia, A.; Robert L. Hampel; and Richard W. Clark. *Kids and School Reform.* San Francisco: Jossey-Bass, 1997. 254 pages. ED 411 610.

Wasserstein, Paulette. "What Middle Schoolers Say About Their Schoolwork. *Educational Leadership* 53, 1 (September 1995): 41-43. EJ 511 721.

Watson, Marilyn, and Joan Dalton. *Among Friends: Classrooms Where Caring and Learning Prevail.* Oakland, California: Developmental Studies Center, 1997. 216 pages.

Weiner, Bernard. *Human Motivation.* New York: Holt, Rinehart, and Winston, 1980. 480 pages.

Wlodkowski, Raymond J., and Judith H. Jaynes. *Eager To Learn: Helping Children Become Motivated and Love Learning.* San Francisco: Jossey-Bass Publishers, 1990. 147 pages.

CURRENT TITLES

ERIC Clearinghouse on Educational Management

___ *Measuring Leadership: A Guide to Assessment for Development of School Executives*, by Larry Lashway @ $9.75

___ *Student Motivation: Cultivating a Love of Learning*, by Linda Lumsden @ $9.50

___ *Leading with Vision*, by Larry Lashway @ $13.50

___ *School Leadership: Handbook for Excellence*, 3rd ed., edited by Stuart C. Smith and Philip K. Piele
    ___ copies of Cloth @ $29.95
    ___ copies of Paper @ $19.95

___ *Roadmap to Restructuring: Charting the Course of Change in American Education*, 2nd ed., by David T. Conley
    ___ copies of Cloth @ $34.95
    ___ copies of Paper @ $23.95

___ *Learning Experiences in School Renewal: An Exploration of Five Successful Programs*, edited by Bruce Joyce and Emily Calhoun @ $14.50

___ *Transforming School Culture: Stories, Symbols, Values, and the Leader's Role*, by Stephen Stolp and Stuart C. Smith @ $12.50

___ *Planning for Effective Staff Development: Six Research-Based Models*, by Meredith D. "Mark" Gall and Roseanne O'Brien Vojtek @ $6.95

___ *Implementing Problem-Based Learning in Leadership Development*, by Edwin M. Bridges and Philip Hallinger @ $14.95

___ *On Understanding Variables & Hypotheses in Scientific Research*, by W.W. Charters, Jr. @ $6.95

How to Order: You may place an order by sending a check or money order, mailing or faxing a purchase order, or calling with a Visa or MasterCard number. Add 10% for S & H (minimum $4.00). Make payment to **University of Oregon/ERIC** and mail to ERIC/CEM, 5207 University of Oregon, Eugene, Oregon 97403-5207. Shipping is by UPS ground or equivalent.

Telephone (800) 438-8841
Fax (541) 346-2334

You can also order online (with Visa or MasterCard) from our website—your gateway to information about educational policy and management.

http://eric.uoregon.edu